On Third Thought....

Further Reflections on Retirement and
Other Things - A Mini-Memoir

George Waas

authorHOUSE®

AuthorHouse™
1663 Liberty Drive
Bloomington, IN 47403
www.authorhouse.com
Phone: 1 (800) 839-8640

Published by AuthorHouse   04/16/2015

ISBN: 978-1-5049-0663-0 (sc)
ISBN: 978-1-5049-0662-3 (e)

Print information available on the last page.

Any people depicted in stock imagery provided by Thinkstock are models, and such images are being used for illustrative purposes only. Certain stock imagery © Thinkstock.

This book is printed on acid-free paper.

CONTENTS

Introduction

In 2012, I wrote a memoir entitled "Retired...and Loving It!!" At that time, I covered every subject I wanted to write about, or so I thought. Then, after publication, I began having second thoughts. Wait; that's not right. I had a second thought, and decided not to write anything further. Then I had a third thought. I understand lots of people claim to have second thoughts about a particular matter, but if they have more than one, how can the one after the second also be a second thought?

Frankly, I don't know how anyone can have second thoughts about the same subject. Anything beyond a second thought is a third, fourth, fifth, etc., at least by my count. It was on my third thought that, since I discovered other things to write about, I decided to set them out in a mini-memoir, as a sequel to my earlier book. I checked with an online publishing company, and found several books entitled "On Second Thought" and "On Second Thoughts," and related titles. For those who chose the latter title, they probably didn't give it much thought. But I did, and I didn't find a single book that bore the title "On Third Thought." So, that's the one I chose; as they say, the third time is the charm.

My 2012 memoir was a best-seller...at least among my family. OK, so I gave a copy to each of my two daughters; but at least they read it. Or so they said. And I've been getting royalty checks on a quarterly basis; however small they may be.

In that book, I told my life story, up to that point. My early childhood (as best as I could recollect), my years in school, my work as a newspaper reporter, my family and my career as a lawyer. I also included personal thoughts gathered from more than 70 years of living--thoughts and views that are the essence of my very being. Not off-the-wall opinions, but views that I believe are based on sound logic and common sense; qualities that are unfortunately missing from too much of today's dialogue.

I talked a bit about retirement, as I had left my last job in 2010 and thought I had experienced enough of what it means to be retired to confidently look forward to years of doing whatever it was that I wanted to do instead of being on someone else's time. You see, when you're working, you're actually on someone else's schedule--meetings, deadlines, you get the point. Alice in Wonderland's White Rabbit comes to mind: "I'm late, I'm late, for a very important date. No time to say hello, goodbye, I'm late, I'm late, I'm late, I'm late." This, although admittedly stretching the point somewhat, is what the workaday world was like. In retirement, you do what you want to do when you want to do it. Life was going to be a piece of cake, or so I thought.

What I didn't realize then was that I was still recuperating from major orthopedic surgery and hadn't had the time or inclination to focus on what retirement really is all about. Now, three years later, I have a much better perspective on what retirement means in all of its manifestations. This perspective will, no doubt, be further refined as time moves on.

I discovered that there is just so much traveling that you can do. There are just so many visits you can make to your children and grandchildren, all of whom have active lives of their own. My daughters love to visit with us, and we with them. But as the saying goes, familiarity breeds contempt. My wife and I certainly don't want to wear out our welcome, so we try to balance our visits in a prudent manner more attuned to their hectic work and family time schedules than our laid back lifestyle.

And there are just so many books to read and movies and shows to see before these activities become somewhat old hat.

After more than 40 years in the fast-paced, hectic world of newspaper reporting and as a trial and appellate lawyer, I came to the realization that I needed to become more active and involved in my retirement years. Certainly not like before; but more than what I was doing. Someone told me that going from a fast-paced life to retirement can be like coming to a dead stop after driving 60 miles an hour for a long period of time. This analogy made sense--retirement can be like hitting a brick wall if you're not properly prepared. I thought I was; the passage of time proved otherwise.

In my memoir, I said that it wasn't necessary to have a fixed plan when entering retirement. I still feel this way; however,

I now firmly believe that it is necessary to stay involved and focused on the present. Sitting home and watching TV is not a prescription for a successful, meaningful retirement. As long as you're healthy, you need to stay active. After all, the only difference between working and retirement is working. In the ideal world, just about everything else should remain the same. At least, this should be the attitude one takes going into retirement.

This sequel to my 2012 book--my mini-memoir--focuses on three general subjects. First, my reflections on things past; second, living in the present, since it's the only time we can live (the past is history and the future lies ahead); and third, making sure that, to the best of my ability, my future is bright and enjoyable by remaining involved in matters of interest and importance to me. As the saying goes: I am the master of my fate; I am the captain of my soul. Or something like that.

So, here goes.

I. Reflections on Things Past

1. Our first post-retirement travel experiences

When I wrote my memoir, I was filled with anticipation and excitement. It was in 2012 and my wife Harriet and I were planning a busy 2013--a cruise to the Panama Canal; a train-and-bus trip through the Canadian Rockies; and a trip to Rome, Pompeii. Sorrento, the Isle of Capri and the Amalfi Coast.

We did the Panama Canal cruise in April; the Canadian Rockies trip in August and September; and the trip to Rome in October. These experiences gave me unforgettable memories that Harriet and I committed to Shutterfly scrapbooks that grace our family room coffee table. We love to take pictures, and we make sure we're in most of them.

The Panama Canal cruise took us to Aruba; Cartagena, Colombia Panama, Costa Rica, and Grand Cayman. The most awesome experience, however, was sailing through the Panama Canal. This engineering marvel was celebrating its 100th birthday in 2013, and Harriet and I stood in abject silence as we passed through each lock, watching the water rise and fall as we slowly cruised from one side to the lake in the center. You have to be there to fully appreciate the technology back then that today permits a huge cruise ship designed 90 years after the canal's construction to pass through. How they could have known then how big today's cruise ships are, leaves me stunned. There are no words that can describe this feeling.

This cruise allowed us to see man-made wonders; the Canadian Rockies trip showed us the splendor of natural wonders. Starting in Seattle, traveling by train to Vancouver and Kamloops, then by bus to Jasper and Lake Louise, taking a walk on the Columbia Ice Field, traveling to Banff, taking a helicopter ride over part of the Rockies, and finishing our trip with a two-day stay in Calgary (including taking in a Canadian Football League game) also made for a lifetime of memories--and another Shutterfly scrapbook.

The site of Lake Louise from our hotel room, looking at a huge glacier in back of this beautiful clear lake, is absolutely breathtaking, as are the Columbia Ice Field and Banff. Canadian football is a fascinating game to watch; more wide open play than American football. The Saddledome--home of the National Hockey League's Calgary Flames--is a unique site among sports arenas; it's shape unmistakably informs you of the reason for its name. In Vancouver and Calgary, we made sure to visit the towers that give a beautiful birds-eye view of these magnificent cities. Years ago, I visited Toronto and toured the tower there, so I believe all I have left is the one in Montreal. Perhaps one of these days.....

For our third trip in 2013, we traveled to Rome, taking a direct flight from Atlanta. This was the first time we had ever been to Europe, and I wanted to make sure that this first experience was Rome. Ever since I read Julius Caesar in high school, I wanted to visit this historic city. What had been a 50-year pipedream became reality. Spending two days inside the Colosseum; walking the paths in the heart of the Roman Empire and Roman Forum; tossing coins in Trevi Fountain; seeing the Spanish Steps and the sites where Julius Caesar was assassinated and cremated; standing inside the Pantheon; touring the subterranean sites of ancient Rome; and walking through St. Peter's Square, St. Peter's Basilica, the Vatican Museum and sitting in the Sistine Chapel are experiences that can't be described. You have to see them to fully grasp the magnificence, grandeur and beauty of Rome; its architecture, art, beauty and splendor. We did our best to capture them in...a Shutterfly scrapbook.

Recently, I read articles about tourists being arrested and having to pay heavy fines for scratching their initials into the walls of the Colosseum. Defacing one of the world's great monuments of ancient history is childish, boorish and stupid. They richly deserved to be arrested, fined and held up to be the fools they are. But during our visit, I did something that no one will ever notice, and it did no damage to this great iconic structure. Here's the story.

During our second tour, we were taken by our guide to the top of the Flavian Amphitheater (if you didn't know the real name of the Colosseum, you do now). At one point, we were facing the interior, with our backs facing Palatine Hill, site of the ancient palaces and Roman forum. I was in the back of the tour group, leaning my elbow against a four-foot high wall, when I noticed that one of the ancient bricks stuck out a little farther than the others. With my forefinger and thumb, I managed to grab the extended corner and noticed that the brick moved when I wiggled it. I made sure no one was looking, and I continued to wiggle this brick, getting a better and better grip on it.

After about a minute or so, the brick was in my hand, with no damage or evidence of its removal, other than an empty space where this brick resided for, as far as I could tell, almost 2000 years. This brick, about a half-inch thick and about six inches long and four inches wide, was definitely part of the original Colosseum, again at least as far as I could tell. Self-consciously, I put it behind my back and slowly moved to the opposite side, to a similar wall about five feet away. Thankfully, I was able to pass the other tourists by leaning on a rail that prevented falls. I certainly didn't want to become another Colosseum victim; there were plenty of those in its almost 2,000-year history.

When I got to the other wall, I noticed a place near the top that appeared to have been at one time the home of a brick, but was now empty. I brushed debris from this area, and began inserting my brick into this space. After some maneuvering, I got it to fit so well that it blended in perfectly with all of the others. I rubbed some debris over it so it would blend in even better, and calmly joined the rest of the tour group. Because this entire matter took about five minutes, and everyone else--including my wife--was engaged by the tour guide, no one noticed my architectural accomplishment.

I know I missed part of the guide's lecture about the history of the Colosseum, but I felt a surging sense of pride knowing that I had altered the structure of perhaps the world's most iconic symbol of its ancient past, without any structural markings or anyone noticing. Aside from my wife and family, no one knows about this. Well, of course, you do now. Whatever part of the lecture our tour guide gave, it did not include my minimal modern-day change in the Colosseum's design.

We also did a side trip to Pompeii. Walking the streets of this ancient city (now a world-renown tourist attraction), glancing over at Mount Vesuvius, and trying to picture in my mind what actually happened when the city's population of about 20,000 literally disappeared overnight in 79 A.D. was beyond comprehension. Yet, there we were, standing in what is left of what was a vibrant, modern city--literally a bedroom community south of Rome. We completed our trip by visiting Sorrento, the Amalfi Coast, the Isle of Capri and a canoe trip into the Blue Grotto. What an experience!!

In the summer of 2014, we took a three-week trip to Europe and cruised the Baltic countries. We arrived in London, spent the night, then took a bus to Southampton to begin a 14-day cruise, with stops in Brussels, Oslo, Copenhagen, Stockholm, Helsinki, St. Petersburg, Talinn (Estonia) and Gdansk, Poland, before heading back to London for a two-day visit. While it's impossible to truly appreciate the magnificence of these many distinctive sites on a cruise--usually the ship is in port for eight to 10 hours--you can certainly get the flavor of a country and decide if you want to go back for more in-depth exploration. Surveys have named the Scandinavian countries among the world's healthiest, and its residents the happiest. I can certainly understand why. Oh, and of course, we made another Shutterfly scrapbook.

In early 2015, we went on a seven-day cruise to Mexico, with stops in Honduras and Belize. We visited a monkey jungle in Roatan, Honduras; and the Mayan ruins in Belize City, Costa Maya and Cozumel. The most impressive of these ruins is Chichen Itza. It took six hours round trip by ferry and bus to get to and from Cozumel to the spend one hour to see the Chichen Itza ruins, but it was worth it. The magnificent temple of Kulkulkan is one of the most photographed sites in the world. That photograph is on the cover of....our fifth Shutterfly scrapbook. And we will make these scrapbooks for every one of our travel experiences.

To this day--and undoubtedly will do so again and again--I look at our scrapbooks and recall these once-in-a-lifetime adventures. But there are more travel memories to make, and that's our plan.

2. Pictures and memories

There are many pictures that adorn the walls, tables and desks in our home. Pictures of our parents; of Harriet and me when we were small children; of our wedding; pictures of our children Lani and Amy as infants, little children, teenagers, adults, wives and mothers; pictures of our sons-in-law; grandchildren in various phases of growing up. Pictures, pictures, pictures.

There are several photo albums beneath the coffee table in our second family room (or what I call my man cave). Our wedding album. Our honeymoon in the Virgin Islands. Our daughters' wedding albums. Our trips to Hawaii, Vermont and Nova Scotia; another is our cruise to Alaska, and yet another is our first cruise to Mexico. And more family pictures; lots of family pictures.

Looking at these pictures brings back many wonderful memories; that's why we take pictures. And the beauty of this is that I can look at these pictures any time--the flashbacks, the vignettes, of a lifetime of wonderful experiences that are today's memories--and make them come alive again. Flashbacks, vignettes, slices of life...these are the memories triggered by whatever tickles your senses.

There is one of me as a one-year old; I was a cute baby. There's another when I was in fifth grade. Recently, I read the great sports announcer Al Michaels's memoir "You Can't Make this Up." I noted with great interest and glee where he wrote that his mother would show up at his high school in California and explain to the assistant principal that he had a dentist appointment. What he really had was a day at the race track, either Santa Anita or Hollywood Park. His recollection, coupled with my fifth grade photo, brought to mind similar great moments that I experienced as a child.

I remember my father coming to my elementary school to take me out. The first time he did this, he told the principal that I had to go to the dentist because I had a toothache. When we were outside, I told him my teeth didn't hurt. He said I was fine, but that the New York Yankees were playing their opening day game that day, and he wanted to take me. He told me that when the principal asked who I was going to see, he said "Dr. Yonkum Studyum." I really don't know whether my dad actually told him that; the principal would have probably known this was really Yankee Stadium. Fortunately, the principal didn't ask for a note from the doctor; I guess he just took my dad's word for it.

We had a great time, and after the game, we went out for either pizza or Chinese food. My dad did this "Yonkum Studyum" routine quite often through elementary and junior high (now usually referred to as middle school), and I was never questioned by school personnel. I think they knew, but I was a good student, they knew my parents were separated at this time, and it was good therapy for me to spend quality time with my dad. Just wonderful childhood memories. (Incidentally, one of the reasons I enjoyed these games is that I got to see my boyhood idol,

Mickey Mantle, play. At one game--May 13, 1955 to be exact--I was at a Yankee game when my hero did something he only did once in his entire Hall of Fame career. On that day, with me sitting in the upper deck in right field, Mantle hit three home runs, accounting for all the runs in a 5-2 win over the Detroit Tigers.)

Another flashback. At one of these ballgames, my dad brought me a baseball he said was signed by Yankee legend Joe DiMaggio. Since I was about eight or nine, the name didn't register that much with me, although I had heard of him. I was excited, but when I looked at the ball, I told my dad that he signed his name wrong; there's no e in DiMaggio. I wonder what ever happened to that ball.

The pictures of me as a child bring back memories of hockey games, the rodeo, and the Ringling Brothers circus in Madison Square Garden; the Macy's Thanksgiving Day parades; and the boxing bouts at St. Nick's Arena. The first time my dad took me to the boxing matches, I was 12. He told me I had to be 16 to get in, so on a cold winter's night, I had to turn up my coat collar and try to act older so I would be admitted. What I didn't know is that my dad had arranged with the arena manager for me to get in. I was so focused on ducking my head in my coat and trying to lower my voice trying to act 16, that I didn't see my dad and the manager hiding a good laugh. Dad filled me in on all the details later, and we both got a good laugh out of it. What surprised my dad the most, though, was my reaction when one of the fighters got cut. I started yelling "Hit him! Hit him again!" I really got caught up in the action. I think I surprised my dad.

Then there were the weekly visits to hotels my dad managed (the Seville and Madison Square). Each Saturday, he would take my brother and me out for breakfast, but a special breakfast of cinnamon buns and coffee. He would order six buns--huge New York-styled buns that were called snake buns because of the way the dough was wrapped with cinnamon in between--and when the cashier was about to ring up the buns and coffee order, my dad would say the six buns were for me; he would order four more for him and my brother. Yes, I was a pudgy little boy back in the 50s, and those cinnamon buns were soooo good. But not as sweet as the memories.

Pictures of Harriet and me as little children, young adults, our wedding photo; memories flood my mind. So much has happened between each of these pictures. I could fill a book. Hmmm, I already have, and here I am still writing.

Across from the wall on which our pictures hang, there's the Lani wall, covered with pictures of her as a little girl, a young lady; her husband Brian, and their two girls at different stages of their growth. On another wall down our hallway is the Amy wall, with the same types of photos. I look at the many pictures of our daughters when they were young, and compare them with our grandchildren's. I can see Harriet and me in them, although Harriet's view doesn't necessarily compare with mine. Family members and friends have their own opinion of who looks like who. It really doesn't matter; what parents see in family pictures is what is real to them. What we choose to see is what is real to us.

I see pictures of Barry, my late younger brother by four years, in his army uniform. He developed cancer while in the military, was honorably, but medically, discharged and returned home to pursue his education. He received his Ph.D from the University of Maryland and worked as an audiologist until he passed away in 1984 at 36. His widow, Anne, and I still keep in touch after all these years. We trade email on our travels and just generally keep up with one other about the things going on in our lives.

The pictures of my brother bring to mind a time when we were both just two young brothers; boys who did what boys do. Our dad brought us baseballs, bats and gloves; boxing gloves and hockey sticks and pucks. When the weather was bad, we'd play baseball in our apartment, making up a game we called "baseball bunt," where the pitcher would toss the ball underhand to the batter, who would try to bunt the ball away from the pitcher and run to one base and home again before the pitcher could retrieve the ball and tag the batter. We played this game in our living room; not a lot of space, but kids can be inventive. We tried to avoid hitting a wall or window, but we weren't always successful. While we never broke a window, we did manage to scuff and dent a wall and knock over a couple of lamps. But we never damaged the TV.

Another game we invented was a scaled down, non-ice version of indoor hockey. Our apartment in the Bronx had linoleum flooring, which can be quite slippery. This was great for hitting a hockey puck. We set up goals on opposite sides, one separating the living room from the kitchen, the other separating the hallway from the living room. We scuffed the floor, and the walls bore puck marks, but we managed to avoid breaking anything.

Of course, our mom hated bad weather, because she would have to worry about us doing damage. She would tell us repeatedly to go outside and play, but we enjoyed the occasional bad weather, or we would limit our play to when she was at work and we were home from school. In the north, heavy snow kept kids home from school on occasion, but because our mom worked two blocks away from home, she had to go to work even on the worst of days. That's when we would have our fun.

We used the boxing gloves in our bedroom. Because I was taller than Barry, I had to get on my knees for our boxing matches. We rigged up a timer and we'd actually fight three-minute rounds. But we made up a game in which we couldn't hit anything but each other's gloves. These gloves were, for us, huge with lots of padding, so there was no risk of getting hurt. I'm left-handed, so my punches landed on Barry's right glove. After awhile, that glove was misshaped into a wad of padding shifted to one side. I made believe I was Rocky Marciano, the heavyweight champion at the time, and Barry was whoever his opponent was. Of course, Marciano retired as an undefeated champion, so I never lost.

Except one time. Barry and I were boxing when he accidentally kicked me in the kneecap. I toppled over like a tree, grabbing my knee and yelling in pain. Barry stood there, counted to 10, declared himself the winner, and then proceeded to help me. This was the last time we used those boxing gloves. In fact, it was the last time we ever fought. He was also getting bigger, and my height advantage was rapidly slipping away. This was as good a time as any to stop.

Another memory is the time we were tussling on one of our beds when I rolled onto the floor. As I was getting up, mouth high to a nightstand, Barry rolled on top of me, sending my face front-teeth first into the nightstand. I felt a sharp pain in my mouth and saw a piece of white something fall to the floor. I reached for it with one hand and, with the other, felt a gap where tooth should have been. I ran to the bathroom and looked in the mirror. I started crying and yelling "I'm ruined, I'm ruined." I had half a tooth missing.

I went to the dentist and was fitted with a plastic cap, since, at 12, my teeth had not developed to full size yet. I had to wait two weeks for this cap to be ready. During this time, I had to deal with less than sympathetic classmates, and my own self-consciousness. Eventually, the plastic cap gave way to the permanent gold-backed porcelain tooth that I've had since I was 16. However, I learned relatively recently that tooth whiteners are great on normal teeth, but don't work on caps. So, while the rest of my smile shows reasonably white teeth for one of my age--thanks to Colgate--the cap is a bit off-white. I notice it, maybe others do, but there's nothing I can do about it.

It is said a picture is worth a thousand words. So true.

The subject is memories, and as I think about my dad and Barry, I would be remiss if I failed to mention the inevitable sad memories we must all experience; none sadder than the loss of a loved one. Well-meaning people say, oh, you'll get over it. You never get over it. Someone who has been in your life from the beginning is no longer. Your parents. A brother or sister, aunt or uncle. Losing someone so close; that stays with you. As time passes, you eventually come to terms with the loss; you really have no choice. While it's very difficult to wrap your mind around the oxymoronic reality that dying is part of life, you eventually realize that life goes on. I don't recall who told me this, but I learned early on that when you lose a loved one, it's important to remember the good times you shared with that person. This helps to deal with the loss. Think of all the ways this person influenced your life. This will deepen your appreciation of the richness of that person's value in your life.

Teaching to remember the good times helps, especially with children having to deal with loss. Usually, a child's first experience is with the loss of a pet. When my daughters were little, we had a hamster, guinea pig, mouse, rabbit and goldfish before we had a dog and cats. When their first pet died, Harriet and I actually had a funeral ceremony. We flushed the goldfish down the commode, and buried the others in our back yard. The girls took these ceremonies very seriously, which is exactly as it should be. We dug a hole, wrapped the pet in cloth, put it in a box, and buried the box, finally covering the spot with leaves. Except the goldfish, which we wrapped in tissue paper for the flushing ceremony.

We know this helped our daughters through this rough time, but they were eager to get another pet, knowing that each one is special, each one brings its own set of memories, and provides the necessary closure to move on. Later, after the girls were well into adulthood and we lost our dog and cats, we had a different kind of ceremony. We had our pets cremated by our vet and we buried the remains in our backyard, with a stone that had the pet's name engraved on it, placed over the site. When our daughters visit, they make a pilgrimage to our pet cemetery... accompanied by their children. It makes for a very touching moment. As it should.

We all deal with loss in different ways. When Barry passed away, I began searching for something to do that would be of special significance to me; something unique--something that I had never done before, and wouldn't want to do again. I was at a loss, however; I couldn't come up with anything that gave me that "aha" moment. After more than a year, however, I read an advertisement that a national beer company was holding a nationwide run for liberty, an eight-kilometer run--five miles--on my brother's birthday, October 12. Aha!! I had never been a runner; the longest I'd ever run was a quarter-mile--once around the track. But, I was in reasonably good shape--I'd been going to a gym regularly for more than 12 years--my weight was good, and I was only 42 years old. So, beginning in May 1985, I began training for this run.

I was able to get up to a two-mile run at a nice steady pace by the day of the race. I didn't enter to win; just to complete the run. For the first two miles, I averaged just under nine minutes per mile. Not bad; but certainly no hope for the Olympics. By midway through the fourth mile, I was looking for a place to collapse. I was winded, and tired. Then, by some miracle, I got what I was later told was my "second wind," and managed to complete the run in just under 45 minutes. The time meant nothing to me; the framed coin commemorating completion of the run said everything to me that needed to be said. I completed something unique, something I had never done before and, from the pain in my chest and back, will never do again. This was my run for Barry. I did it. For him.

Then there are the knick-knacks--things our children made in school when they were small; little objects made with love by precious little hands. Other knick-knacks are those we bought during our several travels. These are spread all over our home. We also have magnets that are on our refrigerator--magnets from every country and state we have ever visited. This is the one type of memorabilia we do collect wherever we go; magnets don't take up a lot of space, and they serve as memory joggers. They cover an entire side of our refrigerator.

Each item represents a memory; a means of traveling back in time to a moment or event that represents a slice of life itself. You see, life is a collection of memories; what we are really collecting are memories. People collect stamps, art, music, books, the list is virtually endless. The owner gets current pleasure or gratification out of a new addition; but there's yet another, longer lasting, benefit.

These objects trigger memories. All of us have various ways of remembering what we did, where we were, who we were with, etc. Just as songs bring back memories, so do those items that we collect. Just as those items noted above are personal to me, so are those items you collect personal to you. We are all collectors at heart. We collect objects; but we're really collecting memories. Try this: look at an object, and think about whether the first two words that come into your mind are "I remember...."

We will continue to travel; it's wonderful to see different parts of the country and of the world. I think traveling broadens perspective, and makes for a more rounded person. At least, I believe it has enriched my life.

When we were planning our Baltic cruise, I noticed that our visit to St. Petersburg coincided with Harriet's birthday, July 6. I told our friends that, for her birthday, I was taking her to St. Petersburg. The perplexed look on their faces was exactly what

I was looking for. "What's so special about St. Petersburg," they asked. I told them we were going to cruise the canals and visit the castles and museums. The facial contortions became more pronounced--then I told them "Oh, you think I'm taking her to St. Pete (indicating the one in Florida). No, I'm taking her to THAT St. Pete (pointing in the distance)." This was always good for a laugh.

We sailed along the major rivers in these cities, and were awed by the beauty of the multi-colored landscape. We now know why the Baltic capitols in particular--Oslo, Copenhagen, Helsinki and Stockholm--are considered among the best in the world for overall lifestyle and general well-being.

In St. Petersburg, we were struck by the beauty of the Church of the Savior of the Spilled Blood (one of the czars was assassinated in this church), the castle of Peter the Great, and the Hermitage. To most Americans, a castle conjures up the one seen in Disneyland or Disneyworld. The castles we saw in St. Petersburg, as well as in Poland, take up several city blocks. To say they are huge and lavish would be an understatement. As Harriet and I gazed in wonder as we walked through Czar Peter's castle and the hundreds of acres that make up its front and back grounds, our tour guide said "Now you know why we had the Russian Revolution." The wealth of what this castle represented contrasted sharply with the poverty of the country; hence, the revolution.

I often joke to Harriet that I've taken her to see the sites of the Spanish Inquisition in Colombia; the ruins of Rome, particularly the Colosseum where human slaughter took place; Pompeii, the site of disaster and death; the Russian Revolution landmarks in St. Petersburg; the Tower of London and the sites of beheadings; as well as lesser known venues of torture and mayhem. I then say "No one can say I'm not a romantic." I'm so glad she has a great sense of humor. My family and friends also have a sense of humor; they better have. If they took me seriously all the time, I'd have a lot of explaining to do.

We love to take cruises. You unpack once, and are set for eating, drinking, seeing entertaining shows, relaxing and touring. Vacations like this can't be beat. What I find increasingly more intriguing is how these huge ships accommodate the elderly and handicapped. Cruising has literally reached the point where physical restrictions are of minimal or no consequence. This is important to me because of my history of arthritis. It is comforting to know that these pleasurable moments are just waiting to be experienced. And we intend to continue to experience them.

There is something else about traveling that we noticed, although companies in the travel business do their best to avoid. It's the pockets of abject poverty (particularly in some of the Latin American countries) and the amount of government control over people's lives. Marveling at the pictures of the beautifully colored buildings dotting the waterways in Stockholm, Copenhagen, and St. Petersburg, we were not aware that the government controls what color residents can paint their homes.

Only one of our tour guides mentioned this, but we were told that this type of restriction is fairly common in Europe. But this is by no means the only restriction placed on property owners. We were told that citizens must apply to the local government for a place to live; there are waiting lists, some people wait as long as 20 years. Leases are inherited, and can't be purchased; only to rent. Needless to say, when we arrived back home, we were happy to have left our travels behind. For Harriet and me, there really is no place like home. Traveling does several things: it broadens your perspective, allows you to marvel at the sites, and gives you an appreciation for what you have back home.

3. My ego room; more collectibles, more memories

Years ago, a family friend who was well into his 80s casually remarked that as you get older, all you are left with are memories. I think about this comment quite often. I think my friend was partially correct; you do have memories, both happy and sad. Certainly there are memories of family, friends past and present, activities--in short, everything that makes up your life. Many of these memories reflect events of your own making; many are those over which you have no control. My friend seemed very wistful when he tossed off this comment; but as long as you're alive, you can continue to make memories that bring you happiness, contentment and joy. And deal with the other stuff to the best of your ability.

Every now and then, I sit in my den and look at the small objects, plaques and certificates that overwhelm my room. I see the precious bowls, trays and other objects my daughters made when they were in elementary school. I have a couple now from my grandchildren. They are of no economic value, but are priceless little treasures to me.

And yes, I have an ego; I would hope all of us do. And that's fine so long as you keep a proper balance between ego as pride and ego as narcissism. Some of my friends who see my "ego room" tell me that I am somewhat off-base for living in the past. They are partially right.

My "ego room" allows me to enjoy moments of pride, happiness and contentment. I see my journalism degree from the University of Florida. Gee, is it possible that 50 years have passed since I received it? Next to it is my law degree from Florida State University--45 years ago. Looking at these--as well as the pictures and other items that I mention in the previous section--make me realize the relativity of time. At 20, looking at 70 seems forever; at 70, looking back at 20, time seems to have passed in the blink of an eye. And so it is.

Below my college degrees is a plaque for serving as president of the Florida State University College of Law Alumni Association in 1974. This was the last year the association functioned as an unincorporated body. I jokingly refer to my year as being in charge of the unorganized (or disorganized) association.

Next to this one is a plaque for serving as president of the Florida Government Bar Association, a local bar association. That was in 1976.

A little further away is one for serving as chairman of the Florida Bar Administrative Law Section--from 1985 to 1986. I also have one for serving as chairman of the annual Florida Administrative Law Conference. Mine is for the second annual conference; this conference is a major undertaking by the section, and the Florida Bar.

Also on my wall is the letter signed by Governor Lawton Chiles in 1993 appointing me to the Governor's Council on the

National Voter Registration Act (the "Motor Voter" law) that came up with implementing legislation adopted by the Florida Legislature and signed by the governor. I'm very proud of that gubernatorial appointment.

In the middle of this ego wall is the Claude Pepper Outstanding Government Lawyer Award I received in 2000 at the Florida Bar Convention in Orlando. I was given this award during the Bar's general session, attended by several hundred lawyers from all over the state. This award has been given annually since 1991 to a government lawyer "for exemplifying the highest ideals of dedication, professionalism and ethics in serving the public as a government lawyer." These are the words engraved on this plaque. Even as I write this paragraph, I am flooded with emotion, grateful and proud that I was singled out by members of the judiciary and my peers to receive such a prestigious honor.

Just below this honor is a certificate I received in 2004 from then-Attorney General and former Governor Charlie Crist noting my appointment as special counsel to the Attorney General. Opposite this wall on the one above my desk is a plaque in recognition of my having been named an outstanding government lawyer--a member of the Legal Elite-- by Florida Trend Magazine in 2008 (and again in 2009). Next to this is the plaque I received for serving as one of the nine inaugural members of the Florida Bar State and Federal Government and Administrative Practice Certification Committee from 2006 to 2010.

There's a paperweight commemorating my selection to the Florida State University Gold Key honorary organization. I was selected while a faculty member of the College of Law. I also have a certificate of membership to the Omicron Delta Kappa honorary organization, also from FSU.

Then there is the large poster bearing the signatures of about 100 colleagues and co-workers that was given to me at my retirement party in June, 2010. There are certificates of appreciation for the many continuing legal education speeches that I've given over the years. It's nice to be asked to make these presentations; it means that your peers believe you have a certain level of experience and knowledge that will be beneficial to the audience.

On my desk are two small acrylic trophies, one commemorating my having been chosen as a biographee in Marquis' Who's Who in America in 2009. (I was also chosen in 2006-2008.) Accompanying this trophy are the books in which my biography appears: Who's Who in American Law, Who's Who in the South and Southeast, Who's Who in the World, as well as Who's Who in America. It's this kind of recognition that can make one's ego run wild. Fortunately, I'm not that type. I think. I hope.

The second trophy was given to me at my retirement party commemorating almost 24 years with the Florida Attorney General's office as Assistant Attorney General, Senior Assistant Attorney General and, for the final six years of my career, as Special Counsel. I was also given a CD of my retirement party, containing all the "thank you" speeches by the higher-ups in the office, and my response expressing gratitude for their kindness.

I also have a DVD that I received from HBO; this was of the movie "Recount" starring Kevin Spacey, Laura Dern, Tom Wilkinson, etc. Here's the story. I am told that there were 193 lawyers who had a role, however minimal, in the 2000 presidential election litigation in Tallahassee. I was one of them. Years later, HBO decided to do a TV movie based on this unprecedented event in American political history. A crew came to Tallahassee where much of the movie would be shot, and the network issued a call for extras who would be paid $75 per day.

When the crew arrived, they began interviewing applicants for extras. Because of my involvement in one of the cases on behalf of Bob Butterworth, the Attorney General of Florida, who also served as head of the Al Gore campaign, I was assigned two roles, one as a photographer in two scenes, and the other as a spectator in the Florida Supreme Court oral argument scene.

Because the movie was shot during the spring of 2008 and the litigation took place in the late fall of 2000, all the extras were told by the costume staff to wear dark clothing and other colors representing the fall season. Needless to say, some of us perspired through our clothing; it does got hot here in the late spring.

The first day of my two-day involvement, the extras were treated to a buffet lunch served under a huge tent located near

George Waas

the Supreme Court building. I was told this is exactly how it's done in Hollywood, so I was happy that I could get the feel of involvement in moviemaking. The first scene as a photographer was a shoot of actor Tom Wilkinson, playing James Baker, Jr., giving a press conference between the old and new Florida capitol buildings.

The second was again of Tom Wilkinson exiting from the Leon County (Tallahassee) Courthouse following a hearing in one of the many cases. I couldn't be seen in either shot, but I could definitely identify my camera, a clumsy wooden structure that seemed real enough to me. I was told to shout "Mr. Secretary, Mr. Secretary," but so were the other media extras, so to this day, I can't identify my voice. But I was there, even if there is no evidence of it. Except my fake camera.

The second day, I was told to wear a dark suit, blue shirt, dark tie and black shoes. Light makeup was applied to my face to avoid glare from the stage lights, and I was seated inside the Supreme Court's courtroom as a spectator to the oral argument delivered by actor Ed Begley, Jr. During one scene that lasted for a few seconds, my face is actually on the screen, over the right shoulder of Ed Begley, Jr., easily identified in part because I was the only male with a full head of grayish brown hair. I was in a movie, and there is evidence of it!!

For my two-day effort, I received a check for $150 less withholding, got to eat like a movie extra, watch in awe as the crew set up lighting and sound, wear specifically colored clothing, go through makeup, and just enjoy a memorable moviemaking experience. HBO also sent me a separate DVD of the making of "Recount," with all the off-camera and movie preparation scenes. Thanks, HBO, for making me a professional actor. Hey, I was on screen and got paid for my work. That's professional enough for me.

Did I get to meet two-time Oscar winner Kevin Spacey? No. The film director told me his concentration is so intense that he isolates himself while preparing for filming. I did get to meet Tom Wilkinson and Ed Begley, Jr., however. Both were friendly with all of the extras. No, I did not see Laura Dern; her scenes were shot on different days and I had to work on those days. The only thing I was grateful for was not getting hit on the head by a placard, which happened as I exited the Florida Supreme Court after the real oral argument in 2000.

After seeing the movie on TV, my only regret is that I was not nominated for an Emmy in the category of outstanding performance by a male extra in a made-for-TV movie about a presidential election gone haywire. I might have had a chance at fame and a new career. (Later, during our second trip to Europe, Harriet and I visited Madame Tussaud's Wax Museum. While in the gift shop, I noticed plastic replicas of the academy award, the Oscar. Of course, I have one on my bookshelf in my man cave; I don't call it my ego room for nothing. Besides, it makes for a good laugh when friends see it and ask for an explanation. I simply tell them it's not an Emmy, but it'll do.)

A few months later---no doubt because of my growing fame as an extra--I received a note from the Florida State School of Motion Picture, Television and Recording Arts casting for a student-made movie--a comedy entitled "The Best Man." As a condition for passing a course, students had to produce, direct. cast, etc., a short movie, usually about eight minutes long. This one was about a wedding gone haywire because the bride was a demonic young woman and the best man was trying to run interference as his brother, the groom, was rapidly turning into a cherry tree. I guess you had to be there; and I was. I played the role of the priest who performed the ceremony and actually had a few speaking lines. This very short movie took a full day to shoot, and I was given a copy of that DVD. There was no food tent and no compensation, however.

I came away from both experiences appreciating more fully what takes place in the making of a movie. What you see on the screen is merely the tip of the iceberg; you don't see what it takes to get that movie on the screen. Days to shoot a single scene; weeks to shoot a sequence; months--even years--to complete the film; hundreds of staff handling all aspects of the project. The next time you see a movie, don't leave when it's over; wait to read the credits at the end. You will see most--but not all--of those involved in what you just saw. Perhaps that will give you a better appreciation of the teamwork necessary to pull off the business enterprise that is the making of a movie.

There are also my Masonic memories. My year as worshipful master of my lodge (1991); huge patents reflecting my appointments as district deputy grand master (2010) and grand orator (2012). These are among the highest honors that can be accorded a member of the Masonic fraternity. I also have certificates commemorating my honorary membership in three Masonic lodges other than my home lodge. Receiving an honorary membership in a lodge is also a high honor, because it is a voluntary act that requires a unanimous vote of the lodge members present. These are in recognition of my service to this great fraternity, and I am indeed proud of these voluntary expressions of appreciation from my peers.

I have patents noting my membership in several Masonic appendant bodies: Scottish Rite, York Rite, the Shriners and Grotto. I was the top elected officer in my Scottish Rite and Grotto organizations. I am also a member of the local lodge of the International Order of Odd Fellows, a wonderful group of men dedicated to helping people. So much of what these organizations do is to help people; their charitable purposes go to the very heart of what is truly representative of the highest and best of humankind.

On my bookshelf, I have three public speaking awards. Taking debate and public speaking in high school gave me the confidence I was lacking. I am basically a shy person; I didn't date much in high school or college, mostly double-dating with friends. I had a couple of girlfriends, but college and my news reporting jobs were the primary focus in my life at that time. But as I moved on from law school and into the professional world, I realized more and more how the decision to take these high school courses paid off greatly. (The eleventh grade typing course also helped immeasurably; I can type faster--and far more legibly--than I can write.)

Next to these trophies is one I got for being on a men's league slow-pitch softball championship team. I needed to have some sports outlets, and for a few years, back when I was in my late 40s and early 50s, this was it as far as team sports is concerned. I have belonged to local health clubs since I left law school; that and occasional walks in my neighborhood constitute my physical exercise. That, and a good diet, keep the weight down.

On another bookshelf, I have a piece of lava rock that we brought back from Hawaii. During our visit, we were told that removing lava incurs the wrath of the Goddess Pele, which brings a life of bad luck. So far, so good; and Hawaii has plenty of lava to spare. Besides, that tour guide told us lots of people take home souvenirs from the many lava fields on the Big Island. The airport security guard shook her head in wonderment as this beautiful sponge-like rock passed through the screening process.

A little further over is a piece of Mt. Vesuvius, courtesy of our tour guide in Pompeii. As we were wrapping up our visit, she calmly bent down and picked up a small rock, told us what it was, and gave it to us. I suppose the gods have no trouble with tourists taking what Vesuvius spewed, but draw the line at lava from Hawaii. It just occurred to me; Vesuvius erupted in 79 A.D.; the Roman Colosseum was completed in 80 A.D. Wow, things were surely hoppin' in southern Italy back then.

I also have a badge and card commemorating my appointment as a honorary deputy sheriff of Leon County, Florida. I am very proud that the sheriff--also a Mason--thought highly enough of me to grant me this honor.

And there's a letter from the Florida Bar appointing me vice chairman of the Bar's Journal and News Editorial Board. Since I've been retired from practicing law since 2010, and long ago left the journalism profession, I am most pleased with this appointment, as it represents present recognition for past performance. I have served as chairman for two previous Bar committees, so it's comforting to know that my peers still believe I can contribute to my chosen profession.

Yet another bookcase holds books signed by the authors. Bob Woodward and John Dean of Watergate fame; Katherine Harris of Bush-Gore fame (or infamy, depending on your viewpoint); Dick Morris, famed political consultant; Claude Pepper; Bob Graham and George McGovern; and from sports, Don Larsen of World Series perfect game fame, and broadcaster Al Michaels; as well as local politicians and media reporters.

Along with my Oscar, I have another item that I love to be called upon to explain. During a visit to Orlando a few years ago, I noticed in one of the kiosks a figure made out of cans--the Tin Man from the Wizard of Oz. It stands a bit over two feet; its body, arms, legs, head and feet are made from different sized cans. On the head is a funnel. Actually, people don't ask me for an explanation; they just look at it, then look at me, and sigh. One man's treasure is another man's junk.

Finally, there are my scrapbooks. Newspaper articles of cases I handled. Articles that I wrote for newspapers, with my byline. An invitation to the inauguration of John Kennedy and Lyndon Johnson. A Western Union telegram from Robert Kennedy thanking me for my efforts along with other high school students in getting out the vote. Cards from Jimmy and Rosalynn Carter for working in the 1976 campaign. An invitation to the inauguration of Governor Bob Graham and Lt. Governor Wayne Mixson. Letters of thanks and appreciation from former United States Attorneys General Robert Kennedy and Janet Reno; former Governors Reubin Askew and Lawton Chiles; former Florida Attorneys General Jim Smith and Bob Butterworth; former Congressman William Anderson; letters from other former public officials; and college and university presidents and officials. I had a letter from Claude Pepper thanking me for heading up his student organization for his first campaign for Congress in 1962 when I was a student officer at Dade County Junior College. I gave this one to the Claude Pepper Library and Museum at Florida State University for inclusion in its archives.

There are pictures with Hubert Humphrey, former Vice President of the United States, and with numerous public officials and college and university presidents and other education officials. There are tickets to the Republican National Convention in Miami Beach in 1968; I had press credentials back then. I was editor of the FSU Flambeau, the student newspaper, and this entitled me to two tickets to the convention that nominated Richard Nixon and Spiro Agnew. Memories flood my mind in flashbacks as I review these items; but that's their purpose: to trigger a memory of where I was and what I was doing when an item was received, an article was published, a picture was taken. Everything in my ego room is a memory, capturing a wonderful moment.

Finally, I have an acrylic paperweight that says "Left-handed genius." This was given to me because, many years ago, I complained that lefthanders are a minority that suffers discrimination silently. You think I'm kidding? Pick up a pair of scissors and note the handle grip; pick up a knife and note which side has the serrated edge. This is serious stuff. One out of 10 is a leftie. Lefties don't get too upset, however, because studies tell us that lefthanders are more likely to be geniuses. (There are also studies that report that lefties don't live as long as righties--probably because lefties are more prone to harm themselves using devices designed for righties.)

Every so often, it's nice to reminisce. I believe that looking back provides for that vital connection between our past and present, and gives us a moment to take stock of where we've been and where we are. It also helps in planning other things we would like to do to further fulfill our lives.

Ah, memories; sweet wonderful memories!!!

II. Reflections on Things Present

1. My family

As I did in my previous writing, I start with my family. My 2012 effort introduced you to Harriet, Lani, Amy, their husbands, and my four grandchildren. (Notice I write "my four grandchildren" rather than my daughters' children. This is a grandparent's right; we worked hard enough to have earned this.)

Lani turns 40 in 2015. (Wow, where has the time gone!!!) This milestone is on her mind; she makes it well known to all who read her Facebook posts. I remind her that these posts can be read by anyone; she doesn't care. Lani is a strong-minded, strong-willed young lady who, along with Brian, her husband since 1998, own and operate a fireplace and grill business in Cary, North Carolina. The business they started about six years ago out of their garage is now a very successful showroom and warehouse operation. This is what two people who share a strong commitment to family and community, a strong business ethic and an unwavering desire to excel, can accomplish.

Speaking of accomplishments, their daughters, Hailey, who arrived in 2001, and Kelsie, who joined the family two years later, are very active in school and outside activities. Kelsie is very much into cheerleading while Hailey is in the band, playing the bass clarinet. These are the types of activities that help mold the girls into responsible adults. I couldn't be more proud of my granddaughters and their parents.

Amy is four years younger than Lani. She is a forensic chemist at the University of Florida, and for several years before that, was a crime scene investigator for the Alachua County Sheriff's Office (Gainesville). Her husband, Frank, is a sergeant with the same office. They live in Newberry, Florida, a small community just outside of Gainesville. They were married in 2005. I am equally proud of them because of their shared commitment to family and dedication to their chosen professions.

And I am equally proud of their two children, Avery, born in 2009, and Connor, who arrived three years later. Avery is the kind of child who, when asked to describe her school day, will tell you everything that happened in great detail. In other words, she speaks in lengthy paragraphs--non-stop, as her mother says.

Connor speaks volumes as well, but my comprehension of what he's saying is limited. Simply put, I don't understand a lot of what he says, but Amy and Frank are far better at understanding him than I, so they let me know what he's saying. The problem is, they're not always around, such as when Harriet and I babysit. Connor will come over to me and ask me something. When I get a quizzical look on my face, he'll put his hands on his hips, cock his head to one side, and motion for me to follow him. He'll open the pantry and look at the various boxes, bags and containers and point to the snack he wants. I'll get it, while he goes to the cabinet for a bowl. I'm sorry for his frustration at my incomprehension. His comprehension is far better than mine when it comes to what he wants, he knows; on occasion, I don't.

Eventually--much sooner rather than later--this will change, and he will be as conversant as his big sister. His parents are in for a real treat. Dinnertime conversation will take on a whole new significance.

Our girls and their husbands are into physical fitness big time. Crossfit is the latest form of exercise. Those of you who are familiar with it need no explanation here. Those of you who aren't, well, just use a search engine of your choice and look it up. I did, and just reading about it wore me out. Amy and Frank are also into obstacle course runs, or "mud runs"--climbing over barriers, running through ice-cold water, crawling in mud, carrying logs, etc., for several miles at the end of which they receive a medal. One of their races now allows for children four and above to run a shorter course. Avery has entered two and finished the less-than-one-mile course happy, proud and muddy. I wish I could have devised a program where people pay a sizeable entry fee for the privilege of running several miles over and through several daunting obstacles, winding up sweaty and muddy, all for a medal that is given to all who finish the run. I could've been rich.

On the wall in our master bedroom, to the left of my side of the bed, are two pictures. Actually, they are poems with handprints above them. One is from Lani, the other Amy. Lani's poem: "I give these prints, less you forget, when these hands have grown, and the prints won't fit ....The love, the warmth, the trust you find, when you hold these small hands of mine." She was four years old then, and printed her given name, Elaine, below this poem. A short time later, she announced that from now on, her name is Lani. And it's been that way ever since.

Amy was six when her handprint was made; this is her poem: "Now I'm in the first grade, as proud as proud can be. I'm learning about how words are made, and, frankly, all about me. I use my hands for many things, as all first graders do. For writing, playing, and wearing rings, and for reaching out to you. So you'll remember how it was when it was exactly this size. I hope this handprint really does make a remembrance for your eyes."

Excuse me a moment. Ok.

My daughters either have or will have the same type of remembrance from their children. What a great feeling! I am so glad that school teachers take the time have the children do things like this. The value of these remembrances can't be measured; in the few minutes it takes to create these, families are given a lifetime of treasures.

Speaking of treasures, there is our "family tree" on my bedroom bookcase. Here's that story. After Lani was born, Harriet and I were shopping at a mall when we noticed an object in a window. It was a piece of wood, much like a limb or small branch of a tree. On the back part of this limb were two medium-size rocks, with a smaller rock in the middle. Eyes were glued on each rock; the eyes of the immediately dubbed "momma rock" were looking at "baby rock;" "poppa rock" was looking skyward in all innocence; and "baby rock" had a gleeful look. This immediately reminded us of our new status, so we bought this object and added it to our collection. When Amy arrived, I found another rock in our backyard and glued it on the second section of the branch. When Lani married, another rock was added; Hailey's and Kelsie's arrival led to additional rocks, joining the Lani and Brian rocks. Amy's marriage led to yet another rock addition; as did the additions of Avery and Connor. The seven added rocks came from our backyard; I used magic markers to draw faces on these rocks. Thus, we now have a real family tree.

Lani and Brian are a nine-hour drive, or a five-hour flight (counting wait time and drive time) away. Amy and Frank live a little over two hours from Tallahassee. We visit them more often because they are closer.

We want to see more of our North Carolina family, especially as our granddaughters grow older and become more and more involved with school and extracurricular activities. Our younger grandchildren have several years to go before school and outside activities consume more and more of their time. But this will happen; Harriet and I are happy that we can see them--and their parents--as often as we do.

Harriet and I are proud that we actually raised our children; we made every effort to instill in them important life lessons about responsibility and consequences for their decisions. And we are thrilled that they are raising their children with these same important values. Too many people leave child rearing to others; the schools, government, etc. Children must be raised; they must not be permitted to fend for themselves early on, and they must not be treated like afterthoughts. There are those out there whose only claim to parenthood is biological; that doesn't cut the mustard, and is a prime reason why, with more and more money being spent on education, the quality of the product-- educated students capable of succeeding in a rapidly increasing technological world--is declining when measured against other countries.

If all of this sounds like bragging, or that I gush when I talk about my children and grandchildren, then I plead guilty and am proud of it.

Since 2012, a couple of other events occurred that impact my family. First, my oldest nephew Marc, and his wife Jackie, had my first grandnephew Micah, which makes me a first-time granduncle. They live in Michigan, near where Harriet's brother, Jim, and his wife, Lori--my brother- and sister-in law--live. Only their son Jeff remains unmarried. I'm not suggesting anything.

Second, I reconnected with my maternal uncle Joe, and my cousin Bart and his wife Diana. Joe splits time between New Jersey and Florida, and Bart and Diana moved from New York to Florida. Joe has provided ancestry information that will allow Lani--who's well into this--to trace my maternal line; she's already done a fabulous job tracing our paternal line.

Finally, I must mention the two beings that preclude my wife and me from having an empty nest. After we lost our last cat in 2012, I realized rather quickly how much our pets meant to me. I missed three little critters--a shar-pei and two tabbies-- scampering around the house, sleeping in our bed, and all the moments of joy that our pets gave me. So, while visiting our veterinarian, I noticed two kittens closely huddled together in a glass cage. To make a long story short, Sandy and Mandy are now--and have been since 2012--a part of our family.

For those of you who are cat owners, you can skip this part and continue on to the next section, because you are too well familiar with the personality of cats. For the rest of you, take note.

Cats are fiercely independent, especially female cats. Our previous cats, both male, were the snuggly type. Not the girl cats. Nope, everything is on their terms. Sandy, a short-haired brownish tabby (named Sandy because of her color), will not allow me to sit at my desk without jumping on it and demanding that I pet her until she's had enough. She will perform what I call her side flop with her head hanging over the edge of the desk and lie there until I pet her to her satisfaction. Then, she will spring to her paws and leap off the desk; she is finished with me. At night, I am not permitted to go to bed until after she leaps onto my nightstand, does her flop, and receives petting from me until she's content; whereupon she will jump off the nightstand and scamper away. Only then will she allow me to get some sleep.

Mandy, a long-haired charcoal tabby (I gave her this name because it rhymes with Sandy) whose fur feels like silk, sleeps in the middle of my side of the bed. She gets very annoyed when I move her. She has no hesitation in waking up Harriet around 6 a.m. every morning to be fed. Both have no hesitation in making it known that they want their snacks and their litter boxes cleaned when they want. Because Harriet will occasionally give them something from her plate at the kitchen table, they have no compunction about jumping on our table while we're having breakfast. Reading the newspaper is not easy when the cats want attention. Getting a napkin from its holder isn't easy when there's a cat sitting in it.

When Harriet and I go out of town, our next door neighbors' son looks after the cats. When we come home, invariably we will find them on our bed looking at us as if they are saying "Oh, you're home. Nice to see you." Then, it's back to sleep. To me, it's as if they are greeting our return home with boredom. But they are great for a light moment and a chuckle. Friends of ours who have cats tell me I'm a cat person. That's someone who loves cats precisely because of their nature. I plead guilty; I am a cat person, and so is Harriet. I never thought that this would ever happen to me, but I'm glad it did.

Make no mistake about it; cats own the home. Harriet and I live to please them, not the other way around. And I wouldn't want it any other way.

2. Understanding retirement's impact

When I wrote my memoir in 2012, I had been retired about two years. As I alluded to previously, during much of that time, I was recuperating from major orthopedic surgery and fulfilling important obligations as a Mason. While I thought I had a good grasp of what retirement means, I realize now that my perception was clouded by the immediacy of matters at hand.

The past three years have given me greater perspective, and an appreciation that today's view may very well be different from how I view retirement three, five or even 10 or more years from now.

Our 2013 foreign travels, as well as visits to our families in North Carolina (with side trips to Savannah, Georgia, and Charleston, South Carolina) and Gainesville; visits to Harriet's mother and her brother Jim's family in Michigan; and my Masonic involvement, kept me busy.

While my Masonic activities were curtailed in early 2014, our travel to Europe as well as additional family visits continued to keep me reasonably active during the first half of that year. However, after our Baltic cruise and our return from Michigan in late July, I began to feel uneasy without fully appreciating why. I began to realize that there are so many visits to my children that they can handle; they have busy lives and we certainly don't want to burden them with visit after visit. I know our two families love to have us visit, but Harriet and I know they lead hectic lives, and we want to respect that so that when we do visit, it doesn't become a chore. We are very sensitive to this, and we know our young families appreciate this. (Although every time we leave for home, Avery asks why we can't stay. I tell her we have to take care of Mandy and Sandy, and she says we can bring them with us. You can't buy or demand that kind of genuine feeling from a young child, and while we don't like to see her unhappy, we are so appreciative that she feels this way about us. As long as she knows we will return--and as she gets older--she's understanding more and more what grandparent visits are all about.)

And there are so many lunch and dinner dates that you can have with friends. They have their lives, too. So with less and less to do, I was becoming increasingly edgy.

I started to worry about every little thing, even things that made no sense. I became restless, which led to irrational fears, which led to panic attacks. What started out as somewhat similar to the fears I developed just before retiring--going from a very hectic and active lifestyle to what I perceived to be a sudden stop--became deja vu for me, although I couldn't figure out why I was going through this.

If I saw the face of an actor or sports star on TV, I had to find out the name of that person, and I would search my computer until I found it. If I heard a song, particularly an instrumental, I had to find out the name of the song and who recorded it. Since

I was now past 70, I began to think of mortality more and more, and that drove me deeper into a mental pit.

I needed some help, and on my primary doctor's advice, I went back to the pain and stress management counselor that I had seen a few times in 2010 as I was approaching retirement. I was told I had classic symptoms of anxiety, obsessive compulsive disorder and mild depression.

After three or four visits, I learned that one of the triggering devices for my anxiety/depression was the visit to my 98-year-old mother-in-law who, although physically relatively healthy, has dementia. I began to visualize myself years down the road, and seeing her in a memory care unit frightened me. Instead of seeing the glass half-full, I saw it as half-empty and draining fast. Although I pride myself on being a positive person, everything I was feeling had become a negative.

There was another stressful event that I thought I had buried, but resurrected itself at this time. A few months earlier, I was at the top of the Florida Masonic leadership team, chairman of two statewide committees. Through no fault of my own, I evidently upset a few people and was blamed for certain actions that, from the directive I received upon my appointment to one committee, I had every reason to believe I had faithfully and properly performed.

When I made inquiry, I received no response. Believing I was the recipient of a no-confidence vote, I resigned this position, and sent my resignation letter to the same people who received the fault-finding correspondence. I was immediately reprimanded without notice or any opportunity to respond or defend myself. I promptly resigned all other positions because of my belief that anyone who is disciplined should not be serving in any capacity, and asked for an appeal. At the appeal hearing several months later, my pleas were for naught and the reprimand was upheld. Since then, I have had no further appointments or involvement at the top of the fraternity that I have served well for more than 30 years. So, yes, this was a most distressing--and no doubt depressing--experience for me. I have to believe that anyone who loved his or her organization--its people and its mission-- would feel the same way.

There were other factors that played a role. The major surgery I noted earlier left me with my upper neck and back fused, so that I could no longer turn my head laterally. For those who like intriguing names, I was diagnosed with DISH, or Forestier's, Disease--a calcification or auto-fusion of the spine. The pain associated with this arthritic condition that necessitated this drastic surgery was increasing-- as was the low back pain, also driven by severe osteoarthritis. I began to feel sorry for myself, even as I knew that giving myself a pity party was the last thing I needed.

During my visits to the counselor, I discussed all of the potential stressors that seemed to be converging. The counselor explained that I was going through a cyclical pattern wherein anxiety and mild depression increase pain level, which in turn fuels the anxiety and depression, which increases the pain level, and on and on. The worse part of this is that I was keenly aware of what was happening and that I was driving this cycle. Yet, I felt helpless for reasons that I could not fathom. I was told not to search for reasons, because they really didn't matter. What mattered is taking those steps to overcome the situation. I was also told not to kick myself for believing that I was smart enough to deal with this, but failing in this effort. She gave me breathing, relaxation and mindful concentration techniques, and told me to make sure I continue with physical exercise.

The counselor also showed me a brochure discussing biofeedback, or neurofeedback, and gave me the name of a physician who specializes in this type of treatment. I figured I had nothing to lose, so I asked my primary physician to make the necessary referral, and made an appointment to see this neurofeedback doctor. Because the counselor cautioned that these neurofeedback sessions might not be covered by insurance, I contacted my medical insurance provider and found out that, in fact, I would have to pay for them out of my own pocket.

I visited the specialist, and, after taking notes on my description of what I was experiencing, he set up a brain mapping session. At this session, a cloth cover to which electrodes are attached was placed over my head. These electrodes pick up brain waves. A gel was applied to my scalp so that the brain waves are properly recorded. After the session was completed, a computer readout showed neurological readings consistent with some anxiety and mild depression. I really didn't need this session to confirm that.

I learned some things I already knew, but needed reinforcement. Anxiety can be based on irrational, illogical fears that usually never materialize. And anxiety can feed a sense of hopelessness, which can lead to depression. The doctor recommended 10 neurofeedback sessions at a cost of $1,200. Fortunately, I had the financial resources to handle this, and I agreed to schedule the 10 sessions. I had five before, and five after, our cruise to the Baltic countries.

I must digress here because as I was going through both the counseling and neurofeedback sessions, I came to realize how stress can adversely affect one's life. As a young man, I gave it no thought; I didn't have to. I attended college, worked two years as a newspaper reporter--certainly a profession with its share of stress (deadlines, importance of accuracy, source protection, etc.)--went to law school for three years and spent 40 years in the active practice of law. I handled numerous cutting edge cases with billions of taxpayer dollars at stake, as well as actions of government officials who did not like to lose in court. Stressful cases indeed.

But I was young enough to handle the stress without anything more than occasional instances of the usual emotions we all experience: anger, apprehension, disappointment, exhilaration, and on and on. As I explained in detail in my 2012 memoir, I handled my assignments--including those I volunteered for--and my increasingly taxing arthritic/orthopedic conditions--without too much difficulty. I can look back now and say that I was never precluded from doing my job because of health issues.

But as I reflect further, I understand that the more than 40 years of school-and job- related stress had a cumulative effect on me. While some level of stress is good--helping to maintain focus and the necessary competitive edge--too much stress can lead to functional diminution. I was somewhere between the two extremes after I retired.

I was getting older--I was 67 when I retired--and what my body could handle when I was in my 20s, 30s, 40s, 50s and even into my mid-60s, was taking its toll. Fortunately, I began an exercise program upon graduating from law school, and kept at it regularly for 40 years. Thus, I had no weight problems. I managed to avoid so many of the conditions that afflict those my age who let themselves go: diabetes, high blood pressure, the conditions that hit too many in their 50s and 60s primarily as a result of a sedentary lifestyle. But I did have something-- arthritis, lots of it. I was told that I was an orthopedic surgeon's meal ticket. Genetics, my doctor said. So be it. There was no alternative; I had to make the most of my situation.

I think there is a tendency, especially among older people, to believe that they are alone in having to deal with health issues, so they tend to suffer in silence. This is both wrong and counterproductive. For example, I wear hearing aids, most likely a result of having to take non-steroidal anti-inflammatory medication for more than 30 years to handle the arthritic pain. Recent studies link hearing loss to long-term use of such medications. But, unlike eyeglasses, there is a stigma attached to hearing aids. Ultimately, I decided to forgo vanity for actually hearing what people were saying. Judging from some of my peers, they are in need of hearing aids, but are putting it off precisely because of the unwarranted stigma of old age and mental incapacity associated with them. And further judging how many young people today turn their car radios to full volume, or play loud music at parties, I have no doubt the hearing aid business will flourish in the future. Just you wait, you young folks who like blaring music!

If surveys were taken of those over 65, I think we would find that a significant majority has one or more health-related issues that require some form of treatment. Rather than silence, it behooves us to share our experiences, not because misery loves company, but for peace of mind in knowing that others are experiencing similar or the same conditions as you are, and that sharing different types of treatment information can perhaps help to better understand the various types of treatments that can in turn be shared with your doctor. This type of exchange is important because a patient's ability to fully express symptoms, pain location and level is directly related to how helpful a doctor can be in addressing your problems. Of course, knowing you're not alone is most therapeutic in and of itself.

When you're ill or just out of sorts, there is a tendency as well to seek out a single solution, or silver bullet, that will magically cure the illness or eliminate the problem. This is counterproductive thinking, and I make every effort to catch myself whenever I'm about to engage in it. I'm not talking about the common cold or the daily aches and pains we all experience at one time or another. I'm referring to the chronic, longer-term illnesses and conditions that affect quality of life. Just as the condition may be a result of a series of circumstances, so it is that the treatment and remedy may necessitate a variation of treatments. It is absolutely necessary that you not fall prey to believing that a complex medical problem will be cured by a single solution. Appreciating and understanding the fact that it will take a combination of treatment forms to address the problem, will bring the prospects of a successful plan that much closer.

There are medical conditions over which we have no control--those that are genetically driven, for example. But even in those instances, we can take charge to make the best of the situation. And there are conditions over we have at least some measure of control. In both circumstances, we can do things to help alleviate the effects. Exercise. Proper diet. Avoiding tobacco. Alcohol in moderation. We have all been exposed to literature that discusses these in detail. They're simply common sense actions all of us can take to increase our chances of being healthy senior citizens living active lives.

Because both of my parents were obese, I learned to watch my weight early on. When I graduated from law school, I began an exercise plan that I've followed (for the most part) for more than 40 years. At 5'9", I weigh about 177 pounds--a weight I've maintained for many years. I can still comfortably wear suits I bought years ago. I keep one suit that's more than 20 years old--that I can still wear--just as a reminder to keep exercising and watching what I eat. Oh, I enjoy pizza, pasta, baby back ribs, fried chicken, an occasional hamburger, etc., but all in moderation. My diet is, for the most part, what it's been since I was a young man. All it takes is common sense decision-making mixed with some discipline.

Make no mistake about it; if everyone exercised regularly and conformed to a proper diet, so many of the illnesses and maladies that affect us would be alleviated and even possibly eliminated. The great obstacle is discipline. Ultimately, it is up to you as to whether you will discipline yourself to take care of your health. If you do, you increase your chances of a healthier life. If you don't, you must be prepared to face the dire consequences of that lack of discipline. With mass media bombarding us with ads on food, beer, alcohol, etc., common sense and discipline are admittedly hard to adhere to; but we must make the effort. Our lives depend on it.

With my heavy dose of arthritis, mostly in my neck and upper and lower back, I shudder to think where I'd be if I didn't have a regimen of exercise along with a reasonably sensible diet. I will need injections and medication probably for the rest of my life, but if this will manage the pain so that it doesn't interfere with my life, I'm fine with this and thankful that this is all I have to deal with. When you're hurting, it's that much harder to realize how fortunate you are. But once I focus on the positive, the pain becomes less of a burden. So much of pain management involves positive thinking and keeping active. And this is precisely what I intend to do. Along with the injections and medication. As my doctors tell me, you do everything you can, and we'll take care of your medical problems. Sounds like a good deal to me.

If there is one lesson I have learned since retirement, it's that stress, its impact and what can be done to reduce it, is something everyone should be made aware of early in their lives. I truly believe that this knowledge allows young people to factor stress awareness into their lifestyles. I already see some younger people taking more time to enjoy themselves rather than constantly worrying about tomorrow. Of course, proper balance is the key, but perhaps it takes life's many and varied experiences to fully appreciate the impact of stress on everyday life. There are times I wish we could inject the wisdom and experience of a 70-year-old into a 30-year-old, but I know that's impossible.

Ok, back to my story.

My 10 neurofeedback sessions were quite an experience. I was told to dress comfortably, and not apply any gel or cream to my hair or drink any caffeinated beverage before these sessions. I was placed in a room, seated on a comfortable lounge chair with a footrest, and told to relax as the attendant put this cap with attached electrodes on my head and applied gel to each of the areas on my scalp where the electrode was attached to the cap. I would then listen to my choice of instrumental music-- guitar, piano or flute--for either 10 three-minute sessions or six five-minute sessions, totaling 30 minutes. When the music flow was interrupted, it meant that that the flow of brain activity was being adversely affected by anxious or depressing thoughts.

After the 10 sessions, I was sleeping better, no longer having either anxious or depressing thoughts, and had come to the realization that these thoughts were both counterproductive and, yes, even silly.

When I completed the sessions, I was simply told to return for a follow-up in three months. No further diagnosis, no further treatment plan, no nothing. I was surprised because all of my medical experiences involved examination, diagnosis, treatment and follow-up. I thought the neurofeedback sessions were the treatment, and that I would receive instructions as to what to do as well as what to avoid.

I had come to find out that these sessions were both the treatment and the solution. To say the least, these sessions helped immeasurably without any invasive measures. Unfortunately, insurance companies treat this form of non-invasive treatment as experimental and therefore not covered, which means a patient who might very well benefit from neurofeedback simply can't afford it.

The doctor told me that the pharmaceutical companies oppose biofeedback because it cuts into their ability to successfully market drugs for anxiety and depression, and this form of feedback eventually leads patients to be weaned off these strong medications. I can certainly understand why the drug companies would oppose neurofeedback, and, having been in two skeptic-driven professions, I must admit to having some skepticism myself when I started these sessions. But as I neared the end of the 10 sessions, I actually felt better, and if something works, that's all that matters.

The doctor explained that the mind, like the body, can suffer injury. When the injury is to the body, there are treatments readily available. While you can't put a band aid on the brain, studies show that the brain responds positively to music. This is why music is such a valued form of therapy for those with dementia or other brain illnesses, like Alzheimer's. The elderly, who may not respond to any other form of treatment, will respond positively to music. After completing these sessions, this made abundant sense.

As I was going through these sessions, however, I also realized that a significant factor that drove my mental state was pure, old-fashioned boredom. I simply didn't have enough to do, and had no significant, meaningful activities to sufficiently occupy my time. I wasn't moving and doing; I was dwelling. And sitting around stewing wasn't helping; in fact, it was only adding to my problem.

I thought about volunteering for various legal aid services, but these groups are looking primarily for practicing lawyers who have their own offices, staff and resources--and being retired, I have no desk, staff, or research facilities. I had proposed to the Florida Supreme Court and the Florida Bar a program that involves reaching out to the several thousand lawyers who are either inactive or retired, as well as those who remain active members but are retired from the government or corporate world--lawyers in my status--and provide office space, computers and legal research capabilities for them to assist others in the provision of legal services to both the poor and those whose income levels preclude them from hiring an attorney. It is my belief that this is much less expensive than simply raising Bar dues, particularly for those who are retired and have to live on a pension and social security.

I view this approach as a win-win situation; retired lawyers represent a great resource for the state and bar at no cost except for basic overhead. Both the poor and moderate income families would benefit, and the Bar's reputation would only be enhanced.

Until this issue is resolved, however, volunteering with a legal aid group is not available for me precisely because I don't have the personal resources. So I needed another outlet to spend some of my retirement time.

Thanks to a friend, I found it in the Osher Lifelong Learning Institute (OLLI) at Florida State University.

3. OLLI at FSU

The Bernard Osher Foundation provides seed funding for over 100 lifelong learning institutes at universities and colleges across the nation. Fortunately, one of them is at FSU in Tallahassee. Osher Lifelong Learning Institute--OLLI--membership is available to anyone over 50, but in reality, the organization is targeted to retirees who want to remain engaged and active.

OLLI offers classes throughout the year on such diverse subjects as archeology, astronomy, baseball, music (such as Beatlemania), history, computer use, cooking, geology, the military, literature, meteorology, photography, wine tasting, writing (such as memoir writing and fiction writing), the list goes on and on. There are no tests or grades; the only purpose is enrichment and socialization.

OLLI also has a speaker's series, book club, Spanish club, walking club, travel club, and a writer's group. Other activities include dinners, picnics, cultural and art activities, field trips and an international travel study program.

Harriet and I have found this to be a wonderful way to reconnect with old friends and colleagues, and meet new and interesting people with similar interests as ours.

OLLI is housed in FSU's Pepper Building, named after the late senator and congressman Claude Pepper. He is a Florida legend who devoted so much of his 40-year service in Washington to the needs of the elderly. The Claude Pepper Museum and Library is also housed in this building. Going through this museum and seeing, along with newspaper clippings and other memorabilia of his career, a replica of his congressional office, brought back fond memories. His museum office is an exact replica of his office in the House of Representatives, replete with hundreds of pictures hanging on the walls literally from eye level to the top of the high ceiling, to the actual desk he had in Washington. It was during my first visit to the Pepper Center that I decided to donate to the library archives the letter that I received from him more than 50 years ago; I felt it was the right thing to do. Further, knowing that I was given an award that bears his name makes me most proud, as does knowing that he did so much for senior citizens, like Harriet and I are now.

Although we are relatively recent OLLI members, I firmly believe that the kind of activities offered will allow us to enjoy the many classes and other offerings over the years. We are so enthusiastic over this that we agreed to chair the travel club even before we took our first class. While I'm not suggesting that a single organization can be the be-all and end-all in the battle over boredom in retirement, OLLI certainly fills an essential need for retirees--connecting with people, and keeping the mind and body active.

The memoir writing class was so inspirational, I finally decided to write this book.

III. Random Thoughts; Reflections and Musings

1. Leadership, and lack thereof

It is sad that in a nation of over 320 million people, we have a serious leadership gap. It seems that our political leaders are more concerned about themselves and financial backers than about the public interest. Instead of leading, they pander. Statesmanship has been relegated to the dustbin. I have written and spoken extensively over the years about leadership, and the qualities that make for an effective leader.

A leader is one who possesses a clear vision; articulates a plan for implementation; persuades others to buy into that plan; demonstrates the ability to execute it; and has a clear view of its benefits to the general interest. A leader is confident enough not to shy away from making tough decisions and acting upon them. If a leader makes a mistake, he or she learns from it, and works harder to do better next time. A leader who makes a mistake doesn't look for a scapegoat--someone or something else to blame. A leader takes ownership of a mistake, apologizes for it, and moves forward. There is nothing wrong with a leader who shows his humanity by admitting error. It's what happens after this that shows a leader's true colors.

A leader is more outgoing than not, more extrovert than introvert, positive, a good speaker, a good listener, able to process information quickly, and possesses the ability to convey these qualities and thereby instill confidence in others.

I do not differentiate between leadership and effective leadership, since one who is in a leadership position but who is ineffective or feckless is not a true leader. Simply put, as far as I'm concerned, a failed leader is not a leader. Let me state categorically that it is a myth to believe that a person is a leader solely by virtue of the position he or she holds. In the last analysis, it is what a person does while in a leadership position that counts. A person in a leadership position who fails to meet the definition I set out above also fails to advance the cause of the entity, and is therefore a failure. A leader is indeed wise if he or she follows this basic principle: never promise more than you can deliver, but always deliver what you promise.

A leader must have the ability to separate good information from BS. As a newspaper reporter and lawyer, I functioned in the two most BS-driven professions. If I was to make it in both, I had to quickly develop the ability to distinguish between the two. It's not easy at the beginning, but a quick study learns quickly. It also helps immeasurably to have a healthy sense of skepticism. Journalism and law require great care in dealing with information. Both professions teach the importance of questioning; of being discerning and careful, and not blindly accepting what one is told as gospel. Always inquire; never fear to ask; and double- and triple-check what you're told. Verify, verify, verify. I believe this is good advice for any leader.

The corollary to what constitutes a successful leader is the ability of those served to avoid timidity. Never be reluctant to ask a leader what his vision is; inquire as to the specifics of his plan or agenda; ask why you should buy into this plan; seek an explanation as to how the plan brings to fruition the vision; and how this will benefit you and everyone else. The ability to ask probing questions of those who purport to lead will help assure accountability.

There are two types of leaders, those in law and those in fact. A leader in law is one who, by constitution, statute, regulation, by-law, practice, etc., occupies an office or position that is denominated as the head, or in charge, of the entity. A leader in fact is one who, regardless of his or her status, other people willingly follow because he or she meets the above definition. A key element that is too often overlooked is that successful leadership requires followship--the willingness of others to confidently follow the leader's vision, the wisdom of that vision, and the plan for execution, all directed toward the common good.

Ideally, a leader in law is also a leader in fact. Unfortunately, we have too few leaders in law who are also leaders in fact. I will devote much of my narrative to the leader in law, as distinguished from the leader in fact, since the former is most readily identifiable by virtue of position.

As previously noted, in the ideal situation, the two types of leaders will merge into one, where by virtue of both position and personal style, he or she will demonstrate strong leadership. This person will consciously work to earn respect by articulating a clear vision and implementation plan; executing the plan through performance, and achieving the goal. A strong leader is one who leads by example and provides clear direction as to what is expected of each subordinate. This type of leader creates a team atmosphere by instilling a strong work ethic, an esprit de corps. The chances for success are quite high when a leader adopts this approach. Unfortunately, there are too few, and their numbers are diminishing amidst the finger-pointing and name-calling that passes for today's brand of leadership.

There are many variations of style for the leader in law, and the examples I note here are not meant to be all-inclusive. Further, there will be varying degrees of overlap; that is, a leader in law may demonstrate more than one form of style. Some may manifest several. As you read this section, think about those leaders whom you have had contact with, or whom you have observed, and see if you can identify their leadership style.

There are those who believe that, by their position, they are entitled to, and can demand, respect; and that leadership quality is to be viewed through this narrow tunnel. This is foolhardy, because no one can successfully demand respect and expect subordinates to blindly adhere to his commands. Respect must be earned by word and, more importantly, deed. There is a vast difference between respecting the office or position and respect for the individual.

Those whose leadership flows from a demand for respect apparently believe it is necessary to run people down or diminish them in their own eyes, in order to build themselves up. They lead by intimidation, constantly threatening subordinates with various forms of discipline or punishment. They don't want their underlings to ever forget who's in charge. The "leading by worthlessness" approach, as well as the "leading by intimidation" method are too common; while both may arguably achieve a small bump in the very short run, in the long run, they are counterproductive. They are destructive of morale-- esprit de corps--and, instead of reaching the goal of a positive result born of a team effort, the result is too often failure. When I see leaders rely on this style, I remind myself of the old adage: be careful who you offend on the way up, because you will meet the same people on the way down. And make no mistake about it, sooner or later, this type of leader will be on the way down.

A second style is represented by those who are so lacking in confidence that they can't or won't accept someone else's ideas because someone else will receive the credit. They believe that because they occupy a leadership position, their actions are those of a true leader and are not open to comment. It should be obvious that a leader who rejects or discourages good ideas from others is not an effective leader. As Harry Truman said, it is amazing what can be accomplished if a person doesn't care who gets the credit. A know-it-all comes across as arrogant, and subordinates don't like arrogance. A true leader is self-confident and willing to listen and work in a spirit of cooperation.

Another variation is the type who promises open lines of communications and inclusiveness, but really seeks to control every aspect of an organization. This is done by controlling the flow of communications among organization members and by giving the appearance--but not the actuality--of seeking out thoughts and ideas of others. This leader is clever in that he believes--with much justification--that his method won't be uncovered. As the saying goes, you can fool some of the people all the time, and all of the people some of the time, but you can't fool all the people all the time. For the malevolent leader, there is this: if you can fool enough of the people enough of the time, that's all that really matters. Regardless, sooner or later, this false leader is unmasked for what he really is: a self-centered egotist who doesn't really care about those he is supposed to serve. It takes an informed public to call him out sooner, rather than later.

A further variation is the so-called "flash in the pan." This is the leader who starts out like a ball of fire, presenting vision upon vision; devising plan upon plan; scatter shooting means upon means of execution; all directed to a goal--most likely an ill-defined or unrealistic one. Usually, however, this type burns out early on, leaving confusion and disorganization in its wake.

Yet another example--and I could provide examples and variations ad nauseam--is the leader who feels obligated to impress upon you how busy he is. He may have multiple offices or positions, doesn't really do anything that a leader should be doing to advance the organization, but is compelled to give the appearance of working so hard and that, like the White Rabbit from Alice in Wonderland, he is in a state of constant frenzy. This so-called leader seems to be too busy to do whatever it is he is supposed to do; he works so hard at giving the appearance of being busy that he has no time to actually do anything constructive for the organization.

You've seen this type; he says he "tried to" call or get in touch with you, or "tried to" attend a meeting, but didn't call, get in touch or show up. He "tried to" perform a duty or function, but as much as he tried, he couldn't--usually blaming someone else or a circumstance over which he claims he had no control.

I've often asked myself whether the person who says he tried to call me just punched in the first two or three digits of my phone number and then gave up. Did he get two-thirds of the way through an email and decide not to send it? Did he drive half-way to a meeting, only to decide not to attend? This type of excuse is usually a lame one--an avoidance technique designed to assuage the failure and convince the audience of his pure intentions. It may do the former; it certainly doesn't do the latter as far as I'm concerned. The next time this excuse is used, hold the person accountable. Ask him to explain the details of his excuse. I've done this on many occasions, to the embarrassment of the so-called leader.

At this point, you get the message about leadership in its many variations. I have no doubt you can point out examples that I've omitted. Perhaps someday, someone will write a book on the kinds of examples, variations, and practices of those who claim to be leaders, but are really shufflers--shuffling off the failure to someone or something else. It will make a most interesting, humorous, and at the same time, somewhat depressing read.

It would serve us well if, whenever we see someone who in a leadership position, we ask ourselves what that person's vision is; what his or her plan is for executing it; whether he or she is able to execute it; and whether the outcome will benefit the general interest. Does this leader have my interests at heart, or is he or she appealing to a smaller group? If so, is this group's interest also in the public's interest? If any one of these questions is answered in the negative, we should proceed with great caution in accepting what this person is passing along as leadership.

To inquire further into the leadership profile, psychologists tell us there are two personality types: inner-directed and other-directed. Inner-directed persons need little, if any, guidance. They can be given an assignment and easily find an efficient and speedy way to accomplish it. Frequently, the inner-directed person comes up with ideas, a plan to implement them, and demonstrates the ability to get others on board and motivated to buy into the plan, all directed toward a successful resolution.

In contrast, the other-directed person needs to be given clear guidance as to what he or she is expected to do. The other-directed are usually quite good at following instructions, although not in all cases. They will generally do what they are told; but will rarely, if ever, demonstrate creativity in the performance. Nor are they generally expected to.

It should be obvious that effective leadership is more apt to flow from the inner-directed than the other-directed. Leadership problems usually arise when the leader in law is an other-directed person. The problems should be self-evident; suffice it to say that an other-directed person is most likely not going to have the vision necessary for effective leadership, or the ability at successful execution.

I have had personal experiences with those who are in leadership positions, yet incapable of actually leading. And I have had experiences with those who are not in leadership positions but who are in actuality leaders in fact because, by strength of character, they meet the criteria of effective leadership who others are willing to follow. I believe you have had similar experiences as well.

In 2012, I gave a speech to the Florida Masons as grand orator. In that speech, I addressed the importance of leadership, particularly as it pertains to the fraternity that is historically synonymous with leadership. In short, throughout history, Masons have been known as leaders, and those of us who are Masons in the 21st century have a heritage and history that demands constant attention to providing leadership in a nation that sorely needs it.

That speech was relevant then, and is relevant now. What follows is that speech in its entirety. See if you agree that leadership is a vital yet diminishing commodity. While directed to a large audience of Masons, see if anything that is written here resonates with you.

There are three unfortunate conditions born of human nature that most likely affect all of us at one time or another. Because they can drastically change our lives for the worse if we are not careful, we need to confront them. First, we tend to become complacent and take for granted the good things we have in our lives, believing-- perhaps foolishly--that they will always be there. Second, we tend to focus on what we don't have, rather than truly appreciating the bounties and blessings that we enjoy. And third, we tend to fall prey to the uselessness and futility of negative thinking. These tendencies are universal; therefore, they apply with no less significance than to our unique and special status as Masons. We can all readily agree that being a Mason is one of life's great blessings; but there are those tendencies to take our Masonic lives for granted, ignore our many blessings and bounties, and suffer the consequences of negative thinking.

To rise above these lapses in human nature that can all-too-often creep up on us and catch us off-guard, I believe we need to do three things. First, we need to periodically pause and reflect on who we are, what we stand for, and what we do as Masons. Second, we need to continually reflect upon the full expanse of the obligations we took upon ourselves when we became Masons. And third, we need to then proceed to live our lives accordingly every single day. Sounds easy enough, but the evidence in fraternal numbers and participation tells a different story.

Almost 70 years ago, the great songwriter Johnny Mercer gave us sage advice that should guide us every day when he said we need "to accentuate the positive, eliminate the negative, latch on to the affirmative, and don't mess with Mr. In-between." So it is with our status as Masons. Regardless of our personal choices in our journey through life, we are united as a common association of men or Band of Brothers in pursuit of the highest of ideals and beliefs, and more importantly, dedicated to matching our words with powerful positive deeds that benefit humankind. This is the goal; sometimes, however, we lose sight of this by taking our Masonic status for granted and engaging in negative thinking. So how do we overcome these tendencies? I will start with a reality check that states the obvious. As Masons, we are different.

Go into any public library, or go online using any search engine, and look for books or articles on any other fraternal or civic organization, for that matter. You will find, perhaps, a few publications on the subject.

Now, make the same search for Freemasonry or any combination of words including Freemasons, and you will find books lining shelf after shelf, and over 750,000 online sites. And that number is growing. This is no accident, for our fraternity has a rich and unique history that dates back several thousands of years--a history that demands of us its perpetuation. This demand is born more specifically of our dynamic value system that is as old as enlightened civilization itself--to possess and preserve a fundamental belief in a higher being; to do what conscience dictates is good and right by others; to share in our respective bounties; to educate others about our time-tested values; and to make absolutely certain that each one of us does his part to assure the passing down of these values from one generation to the next and, by doing so, preserving our way of life. Indeed, as I will point out shortly, the stakes could not be higher in adhering to our Masonic calling and being steadfast in our commitment and our deeds.

It is also the many manifestations of our value system that are embedded in our nation's founding documents-- and in all successful relationships between the governed and the governors--that make our fraternity so unique and so vital. The key, of course, is to take this value system--our moral compass--and package it so that it is made relevant in the twenty-first century. The past is history; the future lies ahead. The only time we can build this bridge from the past to the future is by working in the present--now!! And in building this bridge, we must use all the tools of modern innovative technology, and both think and act outside the box. Simply put, we must pitch our moral compass to reach the particular mindset of each generation and act accordingly with complete and passionate dedication to our mission!! A word of caution, however. In building this bridge, we must never compromise or sacrifice our system of morality. We must build this bridge in such a manner as to be able to raise it if and when necessary. We must, however, never lower the river. We must never diminish the strength or significance of our moral compass. After all, it is what makes Masons Masons.

The building of this bridge that keeps our moral compass intact while making it relevant to the twenty-first century will not be an easy task; but then again, no one seriously believes that anything truly worthwhile or so vitally important is, or should be, easy to accomplish. After all, success in any endeavor is meaningful only if the effort extended is significant. Masons have never looked for, or taken, the easy way out, and we are not about to start now.

As our calling card, we Masons espouse fellowship, friendship, morality, and brotherly love. The reasons for this should be obvious, for we see firsthand every day what happens when the precious and enduring values we hold so dear are ignored or, worse, deliberately tossed aside.

Just cast your eyes to foreign lands and witness the horrific pain of human suffering. Our planet is seemingly more at war than at peace. Violence and turbulence; horrible poverty and human suffering amidst incredible wealth---greed, avarice, and selfishness-- all appear to predominate our globe. And for what purpose? Power? Wealth? Ego?

At home, we continue to see corruption and greed at the highest levels, as well as pockets of poverty and neglect in this the wealthiest nation in the world; and the grave consequences of not adequately addressing economic and infrastructure deterioration and in falling behind other countries educationally.

And it seems that just about every day we read or hear about another famous athlete, entertainer, movie star or political figure abusing drugs or alcohol, committing crimes or in one way or another is awash in scandal. These wealthy megastars and political figures are fawned over, praised, pampered and literally have everything one could ever hope for. Because of this, they believe that the laws and moral code that apply to us don't apply to them. Because, after all, they are special, or so they are led to believe. To these trials and tribulations here and abroad, I offer for your consideration an historical admonition and a stark warning. First, this historical admonition: "What shall it profit a man to gain the whole world and lose his soul?" Second, this stark warning: "Those who fail to learn the lessons of history are condemned to repeat them." Both of these statements warn against falling prey to the weaknesses of the materialism of human nature and compel us to strive for a higher purpose.

Of course, in both the international and domestic conditions I have just described, there is much good that is exemplified by the work of organizations and individuals that ease the horrors of international strife and domestic turbulence. But, unfortunately, the dark side of human nature dictates that we focus on the scintillating and tragic, as opposed to the quiet and good work done by so many. The critical question, however, is that even as we witness and take part in the performance of good, humanitarian deeds, why we have these storms and struggles both around the world and here at home.

I have no doubt each one of us here can come up with one or more reasons why we have such a great divergence of Man's inhumanity to Man on one hand, and Man's extending a helping hand to a fellow human being on the other. For me, however, there is a single word that captures and explains this divergence; a word that takes us to the heart and soul of our fraternity and brings us full circle--values; our system of beliefs that compels devotion to Deity; hard work and a strong positive work ethic; a system that teaches respect for and tolerance of others; of caring, sharing; and on and on. Without a strong positive value system, a person is but an empty shell.

But we Masons know this, or we certainly should know this. We know that basic, common sense morality, dignity and human kindness are neither secret nor sacrosanct. This is what we learn as Masons and what we teach in order to make good men better. This is also why we share a deep and abiding commitment toward one another as well as other members of the human family, more especially our families and friends.

This commitment takes many forms--dependability, honesty, accountability, trustworthiness, and matching our words with our deeds, all directed toward basic common sense human kindness. What I am talking about is not novel; what we stand for are those principles that have stood the test of time.

A strong value system has as its source a feeling of belonging, being part of something meaningful, something that provides for a sense of accomplishment. No one is an island. Personal happiness lies at the heart of a strong value system. To be happy, we must belong to something that has meaning for us--a family, a community, a club, a fraternity, a religious organization, or some other group. We are, after all, all social beings. So, how do we Masons provide for and assure the continuation and preservation of our strong value system?

We do this initially by bringing together men who share a common system of morality that we choose to veil in allegory and illustrate by symbols. A major reason for this approach is that the human mind will retain meaning and significance far better and for far longer if the idea or concept is so crafted. Masons then take this value system--our moral compass--and mold it into multiple programs of positive action, each one designed to foster the principles and tenets that comprise our value system.

We provide for Americanism and other patriotic programs and events. On this sacred day, we pause to recognize and remember those who made the ultimate sacrifice so we can meet here today in freedom. God Bless our men and women who have served and are serving our country in the armed forces of the United States!! We recognize and support our youth through Job's Daughters, Rainbow Girls, DeMolay, as well as Boy and Girl Scouts, Little League baseball, school activities, and on and on. We provide for youth nights, Past Master's nights, Widow's programs, volunteer recognition, the Masonic Home, disaster relief, and so on. We provide Masonic, public citizenship and leadership education as well as child identification and other community impact programs.

And, of course, we hold fish fries, car washes; various types of breakfasts, dinners, suppers; and numerous types of related events and activities limited only by our collective creative genius, the purpose of which is to raise funds for our many charitable programs which are the hallmark of our fraternity, and to help others in their time of need. Then there are the allied and appendant Masonic bodies that do such wonderful work helping people. Because helping people is what Masons do! This is how we bring happiness to others and, by doing so, to ourselves. In its totality, this is what makes us different and why it is so vital to keep this in the forefront of our minds and act accordingly.

While we are a society with secrets, there is absolutely nothing secret about the basic core value system that underpins our fraternity, and the deeds we perform in adherence to our moral compass, embracing all the humanitarian work that we do. But while the principles, precepts and tenets of our fraternity are as old as ordered civilization itself, when--for whatever reason--there is a loss of sight of these fundamental lights of human dignity, we collectively suffer the stark consequences of ignorance and darkness--some of which I mentioned at the beginning of this oration. This brings me to my second point: the need to reflect upon the full expanse of our obligations as Masons.

We--each one of us--can and must do our part to make certain that the light of human dignity shines brightly through and illuminates all of humankind. To do this, we must never cease in taking our moral compass and turning it into positive actions that benefit others. And we must work toward this end every single day!!! After all, we are Masons not only when we are in our lodges or here at Grand Lodge. We are Masons 24 hours a day, seven days a week. Freemasonry, like Democracy itself, while expressed in eloquent words, is given life only by our actions. And actions require work. Masons pride themselves on being men of action. This is--and must always be--the polestar of our existence!

Make no mistake about it; the challenges that lie ahead of us to build that bridge that preserves, sustains and grows our fraternity, will require work--hard work. To be faithful to our Craft as men of action in the performance of the hard work necessary for our fraternity to build that bridge to the future, there is simply no room for those who are content to talk the talk and not walk the walk; there is no room for those who are only interested in self-promotion; there is no room for those who are nothing more than selfish, ego-driven title collectors; there is no room for those whose only interest is in a badge, an apron, a jewel or a pin; and there is no room for those who practice or are the products of social promotion. Masons don't talk a good game. Masons walk the walk.

Masons don't offer or accept weak or illegitimate excuses for failure to fulfill a promise or do a job. Masons don't offer good ideas and then expect others to do the work to implement them. Masons don't promise more than they can deliver, but they deliver what they promise. Masons don't accept failure; they roll up their sleeves and get to work. Masons spell success R-E-S-U-L-T-S!! The Masonic standard is performance dedicated to benefiting humankind and overcoming the evils of human nature. And when a Mason hears a complaint about our fraternity's state of affairs, he asks what that person is doing--actually doing--to improve the situation complained of. Masons know that talk is cheap and actions do indeed speak louder than words!!

Recall Theodore Roosevelt's famous statement about those who complain but do nothing to relieve the situation: "It's not the critic who counts, not the one who points out how the strong man stumbled or how the doer of deeds might have done them better. The credit belongs to the man who is actually in the arena; whose face is marred with ... sweat and dust and blood; who strives valiantly; who errs and comes up short again and again; who knows the great enthusiasms, the great devotions and spends himself in a worthy cause and who, at best, knows the triumph of high achievement---and who at worst, if he fails, at least fails while daring greatly so that his place shall never be with those cold and timid souls who know neither victory nor defeat." This statement by a President and Mason captures the essence of who we are, what we stand for, and what we do!!

We are not just another club or organization; we represent a way of life--a life of personal growth and enrichment and of giving of ourselves to help others!! To these last several points as to who a Mason is, each one of us must ask ourselves these questions again and again: am I this type of man? what have I done and what am I doing to justify so great a reward as being a Mason?

We must continue to attract the best and the brightest that have the passion, commitment and work ethic to be builders--builders of our fraternity, our nation and a society based on freedom, liberty, democracy and justice that shine as a beacon of light around the world. Men with creative minds, caring hearts and kind souls are out there; we must connect with them. This is our duty. Remember, ultimately, we are judged by what we do; that is, how we live our daily lives both within and, far more importantly, beyond the walls of this lodge room. And our actions must exemplify dignity, honor and humility.

In short, it is only when our conduct matches the hallowed words we spoke in private in our respective lodge rooms when we became Masons that it can truly be said that we live as becomes a Mason. Masons are men of integrity and character, and builders of men who exemplify both every day. Each one of us carries the weight of our Masonic ancestry on his shoulders. Our ultimate polestar must forever be: are our actions and deeds faithful to our moral compass; that is, are they good and are they right for the human family? A positive answer to this question will sustain us and assure our role in society in perpetuity. More than 50 years ago, a young, energetic newly inaugurated president uttered one of the most famous lines in our nation's history. I will analogize that part of John Kennedy's inaugural address now because it so appropriate for our fraternity today and in the future: my brothers, ask not what your fraternity can do for you; ask what you can do for your fraternity!!

My Brothers, we are the Masons! Our history unwaveringly demonstrates that Masons settle for nothing less than success or victory. We set the bar! We are the standard by which others are measured! If we are to be true to our heritage, we must live by what we preach. We must lead, for we are the leadership fraternity. Leadership is our birthright!! And we lead by our actions. If we don't set the example of effective leadership, and if we don't practice what we preach, we will be abdicating our moral imperative. To fulfill this leadership commitment that lies at the heart and soul of our fraternity, and live by the truism that Masons are builders, we must act to overcome any obstacle to what we stand for and what we do and continue to breathe life into our words. And we must provide direction and purpose because this is what leaders do.

It is no accident that our Masonic ancestors survived inquisitions, purges, war and demonization. History teaches that where oppressed people seek freedom, you will find the Masons. When there is a cry for justice, you will find the Masons. When liberty and democracy are imperiled, you will find the Masons. Throughout history, the Masons have fought against despots, dictators and demagogues.

And while so many of those who brought such evil to our world now wallow in disgrace and infamy in the dustbin of history, we Masons are still standing proud and strong!!! Our moral code and commitment to humankind transcend any effort to defeat, demonize or marginalize us. We must never allow negativism or pessimism to creep into our mindset. To put it bluntly, we must never allow ourselves to become our own worst enemy. We must never lose our Masonic focus!!

We must treat every challenge or obstacle placed in our path as an opportunity to perform by reaching for the highest and finest in the human experience, and thereby showing the world what we are made of and how and why we have survived for so long. We must strive to rise above the dark temptations of human nature, because in the absence of the strong legitimate moral compass that is the bedrock of our fraternity, there is conflict, discord and chaos. We must avoid these stark and unacceptable consequences at all costs!! There is no alternative to positive thinking and positive action!!! We must never lose sight of the fact that Freemasonry is a gift, a gift of enlightenment and knowledge. And gifts are to be shared. Let me now share with you a wonderful statement from a Masonic publication of who a Mason is: "(a) Mason is a man who does all the good he can, in as many ways as he can, in as many places as he can, to as many people as he can, for as long as he can."

Of course, we can't--and don't--do what we do alone. At our sides providing love and encouragement are our ladies. I will state the obvious: without them, we cannot succeed; with them, we dare not fail. Thank you, ladies, for everything you do for us. The bottom line is that we must remain vigilant in the pursuit of our mission;

we must never allow ourselves to become complacent. Indeed, we simply cannot afford it. History tells us that the price of complacency, indifference or even overconfidence is too high to pay. And we all know that negative thinking accomplishes nothing. We must work hard to overcome any tendency toward complacency or negativity and do what our heritage demands of us both in words and deeds. I have set out a number of actions that are imposed upon us as Masons. These are not options; rather, they are our obligations!!! Freemasonry is--and must always be--a work in progress!!

I believe that if we adhere to what I have set out today and live by the traditional, historic Masonic standard, the risks of complacency and negativity creeping into our Masonic lives--indeed, our lives in general--will be greatly diminished, if not eliminated. And we will remain the "can do" fraternity that tradition tells us we are! At this time, I ask each Mason in this lodge room to say to yourself silently "I am a Mason." Now let your Brothers and everyone else here in this lodge room hear you. Say it loud. "I am a Mason." Say it one more time with pride. "I am a Mason." And let us vow never to take for granted what these powerful words mean.

We are the greatest fraternal organization ever created by the mind, heart and spirit of Man. Our history and tradition are unparalleled in human history. We must live up to our heritage and continue to be the shining example to all humankind.

We must continue to do our part to uplift our fellow human beings who have not yet experienced what we know are the immutable laws of common decency. Indeed, our heritage demands this of us.

And again, we must do this every single day, for Freemasonry is not a sprint, it is not even a marathon; it is a journey of continuing growth, development, commitment and duty that lasts a lifetime.

So, let us now renew our commitment and dedication to live together in peace and harmony; to work together to assure the growth and preservation of our fraternity; to strive to increase our efforts at self-improvement; to share with one another our great moral compass; to accentuate the positive and eliminate the negative; latch on to the affirmative; and by our actions continue to shine the light of Freemasonry into the darkest corners of our planet. This is our challenge; this is our mission; this is our calling.

And our individual and collective success in spreading the light of Freemasonry assures that this will truly be said about each one of us one day: "Well done, good and faithful servant." We are the Masons! We will build that bridge to the future!!! This is our passion!!! This is our destiny!!

Whatever may be the odds; however difficult the task; whatever burdens are brought to bear, know this: we shall persevere; we shall prevail; we shall endure!! God bless you, God bless our great fraternity, and God bless the United States of America.

The message in my speech is a simple one, and is not limited to Masonic organizations. I believe the points I set out apply universally. It bears repeating that leadership starts with a positive attitude, a vision, a plan of action and a willingness to lead by example. Thus, leadership is more than simply accepting a position; it requires work. And there is no shortcut to the work necessary to be a successful leader.

I don't believe I am overgeneralizing when I say that there are too many who believe that simply occupying a leadership position is, by definition, leadership. They are content to collect titles or offices and the emoluments of the position, without doing the heavy lifting that goes with the office. Some may be quick to come up with ideas, but want someone else to do the work, if they even know what precise action it will take to carry out the mission. It is self-evident that for true effective leadership in law, there must be unity between the position one occupies and the positive action he or she takes.

As Thomas Edison said: "Vision without execution is hallucination." Unless the idea is accompanied by an implementation plan, and the leader takes the lead in its implementation, the idea will go nowhere. I hear too many people absolve themselves of responsibility by simply declaring that they are idea people, and that the implementation should be done by others. This is nonsense.

Abraham Lincoln said "Nearly all men can stand adversity, but if you want to test a man's character, give him power." It is important that we take his words seriously. We have, unfortunately, seen people promise the moon if elected to office, only to find, much to our dismay, that the person elected is not the same person who is serving. We have been misled again and again by those who promise effective leadership but deliver arrogance, disappointment, disingenuousness, indifference, fecklessness and on and on. Power can change a person, and not always for the better. Power is a true test of character.

One reason for poor leadership is that the voters don't do enough, or know enough, to challenge what is passed off as fact, or how these politicians intend to carry out their promises. Once in office, these supposed leaders believe they are shielded from damaging public scrutiny, or perhaps they've convinced themselves that they can say and do whatever they wish with impunity. They believe--with ample justification--that the populace is sufficiently naive or uneducated and therefore incapable of rising up and holding their hands to the fire.

If we the people don't hold our chosen leaders accountable, then who will? And if not now, when? If we are to have effective and efficient leadership, holding our representatives accountable is an absolute necessity. We must be vigilant in holding them to their promises. We must keep them honest. To do our job in making certain they do theirs, we must have an educated populace constantly demanding accountability. It's that simple--and that difficult.

There is yet another reason for poor leadership, and this is placed directly on those who make the choice. I call this "leadership and the nice guy syndrome." This is demonstrated by an organization that, in seeking a leader, will look for someone who is pleasant, easy-going, doesn't make waves, hasn't said or done anything controversial--in short, they're looking for someone who is just a "nice guy." So, because he's neither taken a stand on anything, nor done anything that might subject him to scrutiny, he's chosen to assume a leadership position.

When this "chosen one" fails to offer a vision; fails to present any plan or agenda; fails to ask of the organization members anything that is designed to move the entity forward--in short, a complete failure as a leader--the organization usually doesn't look introspectively and blame itself for choosing a poor leader. Rather, assuming the organization even has an understanding of how it went wrong, it will, more likely than not, proceed on the same failed path as before in looking for a successor. It takes intelligence to choose a competent leader; the kind of leadership we seem to be getting sends a message about the intelligence of the voter.

As I point out later in this book, an educated and informed citizenry is absolutely essential for government accountability. Unfortunately, the trend in education seems to be moving in the opposite direction. We must address the unquestioned need to revamp our educational system to produce intelligent, rational thinking people--especially our youth--capable of leading productive lives; and the equally unquestioned need to critically analyze the words and examine the deeds of our governmental leaders so they can be held truly accountable. After all, even though it too often seems to the contrary, in the last analysis, we are the masters; they are the servants.

Another trend I see is the enabling of poor leadership by giving awards and other forms of recognition at the end of an officer's term, even if that officer did nothing but serve as presiding officer. This supposed leader offered no plan of action, no suggestions for programs or functions, etc. The officer did nothing to advance the organization; yet, at the end of his term, he's showered with honors and praise that is wholly undeserving. As Mark Twain observed: "It is better to deserve honors and not have them than to have them and not deserve them." What this award-giving does is enable those who do nothing, and perpetuates this do-nothing attitude to future officeholders and putative leaders. This is not only counterproductive, but destructive of the level of leadership our society fervently and sorely needs. At bottom, rewarding the undeserving for non-performance or poor performance only encourages both.

What is lost on too many is the simple point that leadership is founded on faith and confidence others have in the leader, and not the leader's title. People are sheep; they will follow those who they believe exhibit strong leadership qualities. To this end, it is vitally important to understand that these qualities may not be directed toward benevolent ends. If a leader exhibits all of the qualities I have previously noted, but that leader is malevolent or mean-spirited, history is most instructive as to what can happen when people blindly follow an evil leader. Charisma, vision, plan, execution and support are found historically in some of the most malevolent leaders. I have no doubt you can identify some who possessed the qualities, but toward malevolent ends. It bears repeating that an intelligent, informed citizenry is the last obstacle to this type of leader.

At the beginning of this section, I noted a dearth of leadership in our heavily populated nation. One reason for this, I believe, is the fear of criticism. Those who are willing to take charge and fight for a cause are the ones who, by their actions, are subject to criticism, although to their credit they at least choose to stand for something. A leader must have the backbone and intestinal fortitude to accept criticism from those who either choose to do nothing or may well be too timid or lack the desire or incentive to take on a leadership role. It is far easier to criticize than it is to accept responsibility, and there are those who are more than willing--and quick--to criticize or second-guess a leader's decision or action than it is to formulate one.

Another consideration that tests leadership is the difference between interest and commitment. A person may express an interest in a program or activity, but when asked to demonstrate commitment by getting involved, the interest suddenly disappears. In short, there are those who willingly accept the do-nothing role, most likely because they believe doing nothing avoids accountability. They are correct; but if they make the decision to avoid accountability, their criticism must be weighed against their lack of involvement.

Here is a good example of the situation described immediately above. You receive information about an organization that is looking for someone to revitalize a service club that has been dormant, and you have an interest in this club's particular mission. You are asked if you are interested in this club, and you respond in the affirmative. You are then informed that if you are indeed interested, this club will meet at a given place, date and time.

You show up at this meeting and are greeted with a membership sign-up sheet which you readily sign. You notice another sign-up sheet seeking interest in serving on a board of directors whose duty it will be to consider and adopt policies and put into effect programs and activities embracing the club's mission. In other words, the first sign-up sheet seeks interest, the second commitment.

While hundreds will sign up to join and receive information, hardly anyone will sign up to actually take a leadership role, and be willing to assume the task of making and implementing policy decisions. Think of situations where this precise scenario is played out; it's far more common than it might appear. In any organization, regardless of its size, the leadership represents but a small number of the total membership, and the percentage of those willing to accept a leadership position seems to be diminishing more and more with each passing year.

There is a great leadership void in our country, and unless it is properly and competently filled, it could well be replaced by demagoguery. We know from history that dictatorships and totalitarian states arise when there is a vacuum of competent leadership coupled with a populace that either doesn't or can't (through intimidation, ignorance or indifference) challenge the wisdom of its leadership. Those who exhibit confidence, intelligence, commitment to a noble purpose and are eager to lead the charge are the leaders we desperately want and need. They are out there; we need to search for them and they need to come forward with their ideas, plans and desire to get the job done; and not fear the criticism that inevitably comes with the territory.

At this point, it should be self-evident that leadership is equated with success, because a leader wants to be successful in whatever venture that is at issue. The converse is, no leader wants to fail. It cannot be stressed enough: leadership requires work. No one accidentally writes an opera or the great American novel, or wins a championship. Leadership is the merger of inspiration and perspiration. The following applies to success as well as leadership: when a person asked a great composer how to get to Carnegie Hall, he answered "Practice, practice, practice." This simplistic example is a truism.

No matter how one tries to finesse it, unless a leader is dedicated to a successful mission and willing to work to accomplish the mission, the result will be failure. The work necessary to succeed, however, requires risk-taking and a thick skin. A leader must be willing to assume the risk of failure. Refusal to undertake this risk is a refusal to lead; the obvious consequences will be failure, either through inaction or rank misadventure.

Accompanying risk-taking is the need for a thick skin, because invariably decisive actions taken by a leader will lead to criticism, predominantly from those who have chosen to stay on the sidelines because they are either unable to lead, refuse to lead, incapable of leading, etc. So, instead of leading, or assisting in a leader's efforts, they are content to criticize while offering nothing of a constructive nature.

A leader is neither dissuaded or deterred by criticism. To the extent that criticism is constructive or helpful, the leader will be confident enough to incorporate it into the plan. He or she will proceed with confidence, purpose and commitment. The leader will firmly believe in the vision, develop a plan to implement it, work hard to convince others, and work with others to bring the vision to reality.

While there is much talk about what leadership is, and what a leader must do to lead, it is unfortunately a case of too much talk and little or no action. I believe that there is a relatively simple task that could at least provide some help in addressing the leadership crisis, a task that requires an introspective reality check. All it takes is for each person to ask the following question: what have I done--actually done, not just talked about--to improve, enhance or advance my organization, club or group of which I am a member, or for which I have accepted responsibility?

If that person is honest, and takes the time to look in the mirror, so to speak, when answering this question, there is a better chance that the ball will be moved closer toward the goal line. It certainly beats a failed status quo, or doing the same unsuccessful things over and over again, expecting a different result--which is the classic definition of insanity.

Finally, for those who must choose a leader, don't be reluctant to question the putative leader's motive or intent. Why does he seek the position? What does he expect from the followers? What is the identity of his leadership team? By all means, seek details, details, details. That leader is seeking to serve you. How will this person serve? Ask pointed questions, and accept only proper answers and not puffery or generalities. Just as a leader must work to achieve, so it is that those whom he serves must work to assure competent performance.

2. Florida's schizophrenic politics

As a newspaper reporter and lawyer, I spent all of my professional life around politics. I covered parts of local politics in Palm Beach and Broward counties, and spent my entire career as a lawyer in Florida's capital city, including a stint as state elections attorney and a substantial part of my career with the Attorney General's office handling election-related issues. I also advised the leadership in several other state agencies. From the 1960s to the present, I've witnessed first-hand the changes in the political dynamics in what is now the third largest state in the nation, and my involvement in election matters has further driven my understanding of Florida politics. I have come to the conclusion that Florida politics is schizophrenic. Let me explain.

It is said that perception is reality. Because of my less than two years as state elections counsel with the Department of State Division of Elections, I was perceived as the elections law "expert" when I joined the Attorney General's Office. This perception led to my being assigned to handle the bulk of election-related cases from the time I arrived there in 1987. Although I had handled several election cases before then, the first major case assigned to me involved the 1992 redistricting of Florida's legislative and congressional districts. From that case, through the 2002 redistricting process right up to my retirement in 2010, I handled a dozens of election law cases. So many of these cases meet at the intersection of politics and law--much like an irresistible force meeting an immovable object. It is from these experiences that I have reached the above conclusion; the current situation being the most recent and graphic example.

Florida has twice elected a liberal, Democratic African-American as president; while twice electing a Tea Party favorite and ethically questionable Republican governor who disses evolution and denies climate change attributed to man-made actions to such an extent that he has ordered environmental agency personnel, and others under his jurisdiction, to refrain from using such terms as "global warming," "climate change," or "sustainability." While the majority of voting age residents are Democrats, more than 60 percent of the state legislature, and nearly the same percentage of the state's congressional delegation, are in the hands of the GOP. The entire cabinet is also Republican. Why do the voters support a liberal for president while backing Tea Party republicans for state office?

To find the answer, we need to go back to the 1950s, considered the Golden Age--the Golden Age of baseball, rock n' roll, etc. Dwight Eisenhower was in the White House, World War II and the Korean War were over, and this decade was considered the "feel good" era.

But something was happening to Florida. The "Greatest Generation" was moving into middle age, and the warm waters and sunshine of Florida were beckoning those who lived in the cold climes of the north. In short, the 50s saw a mass migration of urban northerners to the Sunshine State.

From the mid-50s to mid-60s, however, Florida politics was governed by a group of rural legislators known as the Pork Chop Gang. (Go to a map of Florida and note its shape.) During this period, Florida's legislature was divided by counties, so a large county (like Dade, which includes Miami, and is now called Miami-Dade County) would have roughly the same level of representation as the smallest of counties. This gave the rural legislators control of the mechanics of government, despite the election of Democratic governors.

The most visible of the pork choppers was Charley Johns, who succeeded to the governorship in 1953 upon the sudden death of Dan McCarty. Johns was defeated by Leroy Collins in 1954, whereupon Johns returned to the legislature and headed up a committee, aptly called the Johns Committee, that proceeded to oppose all civil rights legislation; threatened to push legislation closing the public schools rather than integrate them; investigated government to weed out communists and homosexuals; and generally acted as a clone of Joe McCarthy, the Wisconsin Republican senator who conducted a several-year witch hunt for communists in the federal government.

But Johns and his committee were clashing with the movements at both the federal and state levels to level the political playing field. From 1962 to 1964, the United States Supreme Court, headed by Chief Justice Earl Warren---the former California governor whom President Eisenhower said was his worst appointment--determined that, as a matter of constitutional law, redistricting of legislative seats was a justiciable issue for the courts to consider. Up to this time, redistricting was considered a purely political decision not within the province of the judiciary.

This 1962 decision was followed the next year by the one-person, one-vote decision that equalized the value of the vote, so that one person's vote was as important as another's, regardless of where the voter resided. And in 1965, the Court invalidated malapportioned legislatures, glaringly pointing out that districts that varied in populations from 31,000 to 634,000 violated the constitutional guarantees of equal protection.

As these cases were being litigated in Washington, Florida had several cases bouncing up and down the federal court system, all demonstrating the tension between the rural pork choppers and the rapidly growing urbanites fighting over political power. The pork choppers wanted the status quo of unequal representation and political control; the urbanites wanted equality of the vote and fairness in the exercise of political power.

Against this backdrop, Congress enacted--and President Lyndon Johnson signed--the Civil Rights Act of 1964 and the Voting Rights Act (VRA) of 1965. The 1964 law prohibited discrimination based on race, color, religion, sex or national origin. (It is reported--but there is no written confirmation-- that at the time Johnson signed the civil rights law, he said that he had just handed the south to the Republican Party over the ensuing 50-year period. If he didn't say this, then it's a matter of urban legend; if he did, he was most prophetic.)

The 1965 voting rights law provided for mass enfranchisement of racial minorities, especially in the south. At the time of its passage, the Justice Department considered it to be the most effective piece of civil rights legislation ever enacted.

The VRA required certain jurisdictions that had a history of discrimination to submit any changes in voting laws, practices, standards or procedures to the federal Department of Justice or the United States District Court for the District of Columbia for review and preclearance before any change could take effect. Because Florida had five counties that issued English-only voting information, these five counties (Hendry, Hardee, Hillsborough, Collier and Monroe) were included in this preclearance requirement by the justice department. (Although the law provides for this submission option, the justice department claimed primacy of review under the legal principal that administrative agencies have primary jurisdiction, and vowed to oppose with every legal weapon available, any effort to have the federal court assume jurisdiction.) (From 1987 to 2007, I was responsible for preparing the submission of election-related legislation to the Department of Justice for preclearance review.)

Because all general legislation impacts the entire state, all legislation necessarily encompassed these five counties. And because Florida law requires a uniform system of elections, an executive policy decision was made to submit all legislation in its totality for preclearance. In other words, Florida decided to include every enactment that impacted voting even as the federal government limited its review only insofar as it affected these five counties. My disagreement with this interpretation manifested a lone voice in the wilderness. (Note: This preclearance requirement was based on a voting coverage formula enacted in 1965 and updated in 1970 and 1975. In 2013, the Supreme Court invalidated the coverage formula as out of date and therefore unconstitutional. That decision effectively ended the preclearance requirement.)

The VRA also prohibits any state or local government from imposing any voting law that results in discrimination against language or racial minorities, and outlaws literacy tests and other similar Draconian devices that were historically used to disenfranchise racial minorities. However, in 1980, the Supreme Court ruled that in order to prove a violation of this law, a challenger to a voting act had to prove that it was passed and enforced for a deliberate, intentional purpose. This standard is among the highest of evidentiary burdens; one almost impossible to prove. How does one prove what's in the mind of a legislator?

As a result of this decision, Congress amended the VRA in 1982 to provide that a challenger can prove a violation of federal law if the evidence establishes that, in the totality of the circumstances, the action being challenged has the result of denying a racial or language minority of an equal opportunity to participate in the political process and elect candidates of their choice. Thus, the proof required to establish a voting rights act violation shifted markedly from intentional discrimination to a lesser standard of demonstrating a disparity or unequal adverse impact of a voting law on minorities.

In 1986, the United States Supreme Court issued a decision that serves as a blueprint for proving a voting rights act violation under these amendments, setting out a three-prong evidentiary test that must be met, followed by proof that in the "totality of the circumstances"--a nine-step inquiry directed to electoral history, campaign strategies, voting patterns, minority access and success--data designed to give a full picture of minority involvement in the political process--that minorities were blocked from participating in the political process and therefore unable to elect candidates of their choice. Stripped of its gloss, if a minority group could show that majority voting patterns blocked this group from electing their own candidates, a violation of federal law could be established.

(Now, here's the unspoken thrust of this litigation. If black voters repeatedly voted for black candidates, while white voters just as repeatedly voted for white candidates, a voting act violation could be proven. While representing that black voters could prefer a white candidate, and using as examples democratic candidates for president and Florida governor, in none of those elections was a black candidate on the ballot. Little, if any, election data showed black voting patterns in which blacks preferred white candidates over black candidates.)

The election litigation described above that began in 1962 and ended in 1967 at both the state and federal levels paved the way for Florida to adopt in 1968 a specialized process of redistricting the state legislature every 10 years in the first even-numbered year following the decennial census. This process calls for the legislature to adopt a joint resolution of redistricting, which is presented to the Attorney General for submission to the Florida Supreme Court for a judgment approving the plan. The Supreme Court, once it receives the plan, invites interested parties to participate and sets a schedule of activities leading to argument and finally a decision on the submitted plan. This constitutional process thus involves all three branches of state government.

While the redistricting processes in 1972 and 1982--all conducted under the state constitutional method for adopting a legislative plan (congressional redistricting plans are adopted in the same manner as any piece of legislation--majority vote of both houses and submission to the governor for his action)--were relatively uneventful, the anticipation of the 1992 cycle took center stage.

In passing, the only significant point of the 1982 effort was the legislature's adoption of a single-member district plan. Up to this time, Florida's districts were multi-member, meaning more than one legislator could be elected from the same district. As districts generally ran along county lines, a large county would have several legislators, small counties would have one. (It is noted that Florida's constitution still allows the legislature to opt for multi-member legislative districts; however, from a practical standpoint, the odds of this happening are non-existent.)

The confluence of the 1982 amendments to the Voting Rights Act, the United States Supreme Court's 1986 blueprint for litigation under these amendments, and the significance of single-member districts led to the most litigious redistricting cycle in Florida history in 1992.

It is important to remember that redistricting is arguably the most political of political processes. Empowering the legislature to draw legislative and congressional districts is in reality empowering its members to engage in self-preservation; they are drawing their own districts, or those of their immediate successors and/or staunch representational supporters. The party in power in the legislature controls the redistricting process. Which party do you think the legislature will do its best to help?

It is also important to note who was in the White House and which political party ran the United States Justice Department during these critical times. In 1982, Ronald Reagan was in the White House; in 1992, George Bush was president. The Justice Department was in the hands of the GOP during the critical period of 1981 to 2003.

Now, why would the GOP have such a great interest in assuring voting and representational equality for minorities? Stay tuned.

There is no doubt the political parties were well aware of the significance of the 1992 process years before it was undertaken.

In 1988, the legislative leadership appointed committees that held hearings throughout the state. Both political parties retained election and legal experts to help assure that the process was fair; that is, favorable to their particular interests.

The Bush Justice Department, through its civil rights office, chimed in with a directive that the Voting Rights Act required legislatures to maximize the drawing of minority districts; the unwavering message being that if a majority-minority district could be drawn, it had to be drawn or the result would be a violation of federal law. This maximization mantra drove the entire redistricting process. (Parenthetically, I never truly understood this designation of majority-minority districts. If a district is majority African-American or Hispanic, then by definition the majority of those who reside in that district are not a minority in that district. However, because African-Americans and Hispanics are minorities in terms of state and national voting age population, they are so referred to even if they represent a majority in their districts. Whether this will change should a state become majority African-American or Hispanic remains to be seen.)

The first legal shot was fired on the first day of the 1992 legislative session when leading republicans filed a lawsuit in federal court in Tallahassee claiming that the then-existing 1982 plan was unconstitutional, and asking the court to adopt a plan that conformed to constitutional and VRA requirements as driven by the justice department's maximization mandate.

Meanwhile, the legislature, at the conclusion of its 60-day session, was unable to adopt a plan, leading the plaintiffs in federal court to ask that it assume control over the process and adopt a valid plan.

Not to be outdone, a special legislative session was convened and, after eight days, a plan was adopted and duly presented to the state Supreme Court. The federal plaintiffs, however, asked the federal court to remove the state court action to the federal court, maintaining that the Supreme Court wasn't constitutionally able to conduct the kind of inquiry that federal law required.

While this ping-pong match between the federal and state courts was playing out, the Justice Department weighed in. You recall that one of the VRA's provisions requires that legislation affecting certain jurisdictions has to be submitted to the federal agency for its review and preclearance. So it was with the plan presented to the state Supreme Court by the Attorney General. The DOJ approved the plan, with a single exception regarding one of the counties under the agency's jurisdiction.

While the state Supreme Court eventually adopted a remedial plan to address the objection, recall that the overriding consideration of the DOJ-required maximization of minority districts drove the eventual outcome.

This is what happened. Districts, particularly those in south Florida and in the Jacksonville area, were drawn in such a way as to concentrate as many minority voters in as few districts as possible. This assured minorities of representation, but it removed minority voters from adjacent or surrounding districts in sufficient numbers so as to render them non-competitive for minorities and safe for Republicans.

Thus, while minorities attained greater assured representation, they gave up whatever competitive edge they might have had in nearby districts. This process of packing minorities into few districts led to bleaching of those other districts--which is exactly what the GOP wanted because, by packing Democratic voters in fewer districts, it removed them from surrounding or adjacent districts, thereby making them safe for Republicans.

What is so remarkable about this is that the groups that fought for maximization of minority districts--the NAACP, Lawyers Committee for Civil Rights Under Law, People for the American Way, League of United Latin American Citizens--are predominantly liberal Democratic organizations. Was their fixation on creating safe minority districts blinding them to the bleaching of surrounding districts, thereby sacrificing any competitive strength they may have had in these other districts, which empowered the Republican Party?

Although the GOP was assured of future electoral success, it--apparently with a nothing-to-lose attitude--nevertheless pressed for even greater political strength by taking its case to the United States Supreme Court. In 1994, that Court decided that there was no violation of federal law because the degree of minority representation was roughly proportional to minority representation in the general public. Most significantly, however, the Court ruled that maximization of minority districts was not required in order to avoid a VRA violation.

By then, however, the paste was out of the tube. The strong minority districts--and the plan substantially favorable to the GOP--were firmly in place, and any future effort to reduce their number presumably would be met with a lawsuit under the VRA, since this law specifically prohibits any regression of minority representation. The Republican Party would certainly argue that any diminution of minority representation--which would increase the Democratic Party's chances in surrounding districts--would constitute illegal regression. This position presumably keeps the GOP legislative majority well protected. Of course, whether it is illegal regression of minority voters if, for example, a 58 percent minority district were reduced to 52 percent, with the remaining six percent spread to adjacent counties to make them more competitive for minorities, may now be an open question.

This is so because the Supreme Court has ruled that it may be illegal to have too many blacks packed or clustered in one district at the expense of others. This decision represents a reversal of sorts from previous decades when the federal government compelled mostly southern states to create majority-minority districts more likely to elect black legislators. Now, the high court said the Voting Rights Act might not require these districts to be packed with minorities if by doing so race becomes a predominant factor in effectively removing minorities from adjoining or surrounding districts. Thus, the question seems to be: at what point does the assignment of blacks to a particular district become too many to satisfy the Voting Rights Act? And if black voters are removed from a majority-minority district, at what point does the reduction of black voters in that district become a violation of the federal law? The answer to these questions may well be found in proof that race was the predominant factor in the decision-making process. However, these questions are, of course, for another day.

The seminal question following the 1992 process is: did the Democrats know what the effect would be of creating these majority-minority districts in the long run? And did the groups representing the minority interests similarly appreciate the long-term effect of their advocacy?

A snippet from the Florida Supreme Court's last decision for the 1992 cycle is most telling:

> The dissenters [the groups previously mentioned] correctly point out that in creating a stronger minority district the influence of the minority voters in the adjoining districts is reduced. However, the Justice Department seems to interpret the Voting Rights Act as favoring the creation of more districts in which minorities have the opportunity to elect minority candidates than

the creation of more districts in which minorities have greater influence.

Recall that the Justice Department was in Republican hands. It is said that politics makes strange bedfellows; that relationships are formed by those desirous of achieving a political end, even though these people may have nothing, or very little, in common. The redistricting process best exemplifies this. There are those who firmly believe that the GOP entered into an alliance with the NAACP and the legislative minority caucus to craft safe minority districts that would bring about a GOP supermajority. Whether or not this was the case, the results certainly speak for themselves insofar as redistricting plans are concerned, since they enhance minority representation while simultaneously assuring a strong GOP majority in the legislature.

However, when Democrats come out in support of plans that increase black voters' chances of electing preferred candidates even when they are highly beneficial to the GOP; when conservative commentators blast a GOP-controlled Department of Justice; and when black legislative caucuses support GOP-led plans to increase minority representation by packing districts, there is much support for the strange bedfellows tag.

I believe all the players in the process well knew the long-term consequences to the Democrats, but the GOP was most successful in literally turning the Democratic Party on itself. The Republicans had to know that some groups strongly supported safe minority districts, even at the expense of becoming a non-factor in surrounding districts. In short, for them, the bird in the hand was worth more than two in the bush.

More than 20 years have now passed since this landmark effort was undertaken, and the fruits of the GOP's efforts are most apparent. With a legislature and congressional delegation far exceeding relative percentages to the population as a whole, the GOP doesn't really have to worry about minority representation or Democratic policy proposals in order to govern. If a Democrat should become governor in the near future, he or she will be dealing with a strong Republican legislature, and a Supreme Court that will be the product of a Republican administration.

Recently, in an effort to counter the effects of the 1992 process, the Florida voters overwhelmingly passed what is known as the Fair Districts Amendments, requiring future plans not be drawn to favor or disfavor incumbents or political parties, among other things. The real purpose of these amendments is to, in effect, return the state to its pre-1992 representational status. In short, the Democrats want to accomplish the impossible by putting the paste back in the tube. Considering the high court's 2015 decision on minority districts in Alabama, it may just be possible to accomplish the impossible.

Following the 2002 and 2012 plans, which further cemented the supermajorities in the legislative and congressional plans, litigation was initiated by the Fair Districts proponents, claiming that the 2012 legislative plan was the product of pure partisan politics. The trial court found that politics indeed played a substantial role in producing a GOP-favored plan, but only invalidated a small part of the legislative plan. The legislature jiggled a few boundaries and the court provisionally approved this remedy, which had no effect on the composition of the Florida legislature.

The case remains heavily litigated; the Fair District proponents maintain that the plan in place is the product of impermissible political gerrymandering. However, the United States Supreme Court, after ruling in 1986 that political gerrymandering presented an issue for the courts, reversed itself in 2004 and ruled that political gerrymandering is not a question for the courts because there are no judicially manageable standards or benchmarks from which to measure when a redistricting plan is illegally politically gerrymandered. The question remains whether the Fair Districts Amendments provide the required "judicially manageable standards" from which a court could determine whether a plan constitutes illegal partisan political gerrymandering. Further, there may be a relationship between these amendments and the Supreme Court's decision that it may be a violation of the Voting Rights Act to pack too many black voters into a single district at the expense of others.

Meanwhile, the Democratic Party awaits 2018 when a Constitution Revision Commission is required to be appointed and whose recommendations for changes to the constitution go directly to the ballot for presentation to the voters. Of course, the membership of this commission will be selected predominantly by GOP leaders.

In 1992, one of the Florida Supreme Court justices recommended that the process be taken out of the legislature's hands and turned over to a commission. It is possible a suggestion such as this will be resurrected before this 2018 revision commission; moreover, the Democratic Party leadership has already represented that it will undertake a more aggressive stance during the next redistricting process in 2022.

However, the reality is that, as for any proposed amendment to the constitution, adoption requires a 60 percent favorable majority vote. What are the chances of such an amendment passing in the face of strong opposition by the Republican Party arguing that such an amendment would remove the process from the people's elected representatives? And what are the chances of a Constitution Revision Commission--whose members will be predominantly GOP appointees--voting to allow such an amendment to appear on the ballot in the first place?

As for the upcoming redistricting cycle, do the Democrats expect a Republican-controlled legislature to lessen its control of both chambers in order to favor the Democrats? Recall the argument that under the current interpretation of the VRA, any attempt to reduce minority representation is a violation. Whether this argument retains its vitality in light of more recent voting rights pronouncements from the Supreme Court remains to be seen. Nevertheless, it can be readily presumed that the

GOP will object to any diminution of minority representation in the current majority-minority districts--even one enhancing the prospects for minority representation in surrounding or adjacent districts--as violating the VRA. The anticipated litigation on this point should be most profound and far-reaching.

In law, as in so many other disciplines, once you believe the last word on a subject has been uttered, another follows that throws the dialogue into chaos. Such appears to be the case with regard to minority voting rights.

3. Economic inequality and affirmative action

I discussed this subject in greater detail in my 2012 book, but events since then have only sharpened my concerns.

From a purely economic standpoint, my wife and I are indeed fortunate. We both spent many years as employees of county and state government, respectively. Harriet put in 37 years in the Leon County school system as an elementary grade school teacher; I spent more than 32 years as a state government lawyer. We both have a pension and social security as our sources of income, with a sufficient nest egg through conservative investments so that we are not unduly exposed to the vagaries of the stock market.

But too many others are not as fortunate, and the current political tide seems unalterably moving toward diminishing social security benefits and reducing or eliminating pensions, both public and private, which will certainly hurt those less fortunate.

While there are examples of pension abuse--pensioners realizing six-figure annual income from their pensions--the present political trend seems hell-bent on throwing out the baby with the bathwater.

For too many, social security is the only source of income for retirees. When this post-Depression legislation became law, it was never meant to be the sole source of a retiree's income. Similarly, no pension--especially one paid by taxpayers' dollars--should be a sole source of a retiree's income. But, with pensions--especially for elected and high ranking appointed officers, and highly skilled and other well-paid employees--at six figures (with some well into six figures), the focus seems to be on these exorbitant pensions as the basis for ending pensions for everyone. Thus, the small example of putative abuse is used as the reason for termination.

In the interest of full disclosure, I am a registered, lifelong Democrat. This, however, does not make me a liberal, because--although it upsets the mindset of some of my conservative colleagues--not all Democrats are liberal. There is such a thing as a moderate Democrat; that's me. I believe in helping those who help themselves; I don't believe in handouts for the sake of handouts. I believe in personal responsibility, and facing consequences for one's actions. I don't believe in giving the wealthy tax breaks under the rubric that these breaks will create jobs and stimulate the economy. This is, at best, disingenuous; the trickle-down theory of economics has proven to be, in the words of George Bush I, "voodoo economics."

I don't believe that the super-wealthy should accumulate greater wealth at the expense of the middle class. Those who are poor through no fault of their own should have a safety net available until they get back on their feet, and there should be a means for them to do so, but those on the receiving end must take charge in helping themselves. After all, as the adage goes: "God helps those who help themselves."

Since businesses hire illegal immigrants anyway, and there are illegal immigrants in the country who are contributing to the common good, paying their taxes and raising children born in this country who will also contribute to society, there should be an immigration policy that makes sense in light of existing realities; this contemplates some form of amnesty.

If these sound unreasonable or nothing more than "old-fashioned liberalism," then you don't understand what I said immediately above.

The assault on social security and pensions as retiree safety nets is nearsighted, wrongheaded and potentially disastrous. A simple understanding of our nation's history bears this out.

Those who want to do away with social security and pensions need only to look back to a time when there was neither. Go back to the post-Civil War period, the period of the Second Industrial Revolution; the Gilded Age. For almost 50 years, those who lived through even a part of this period witnessed the accumulation of great wealth, unprecedented expansion, new opportunities in business, and standardization, which in turn led to the dichotomy between skilled and unskilled workers. It fed into the Roaring '20s and the age of mass migration, mostly of economically and politically depressed Europeans seeking a better life in America. It was a period that gave us such industrial giants as Andrew Carnegie, John D. Rockefeller, Cornelius Vanderbilt, John Jacob Astor, Henry Flagler, J.P.

Morgan, Andrew Mellon and others who moved the country along the road of progress--at a price.

The Gilded Age was also a time of extreme poverty, deep depression, and rampant economic insecurity. Sweat shops. Extremely dangerous working conditions. Long hours for low pay. No compensation for job-related injuries. Child labor abuses. And on and on. It was a time of great monopolies and the accumulation of unprecedented wealth into the hands of a few who, although called the captains of industry by some, were called Robber Barons by others.

This Second Industrial Revolution came to a screeching halt in 1929 when the stock market crash ushered in the Great Depression.

Earlier economic recessions in the 1870s and 1890s should have sent a clear warning of what could well happen as a consequence of rampant speculation and unchecked markets, but any such warning fell on deaf ears. The country was far too interested in the Roaring '20s lifestyle to pay attention to possible economic disaster until it was too late for too many.

Flash forward to the end of the 1990s and early 21st century. Hear the words of those in positions of power and authority rail against those who receive a pension and social security benefits. Read the stories about private companies doing away with pension plans; governments in several states seeking to do likewise, while those in power seek to cut social security benefits.

They tell us that these systems need to be "reformed," but what they really mean is the elimination of any vestige of any economic safety net provided by the government. Anytime we hear government officials in power tell us that reform is needed, you can bet the so-called reform is designed to benefit those who support these officials. We should indeed view such efforts with skepticism as to the motives and purposes of this reform.

For future retirees, these reformists maintain that economic security will be based on sound investments in the stock market rather than the handout. Lost in this false "either-or" proposition is the fact that neither pensions nor social security are handouts. Further, we need look only to 2008 to know how secure and safe these investments can be. That the government won't even consider guaranteeing any protection for market investments that go sour should send an unmistakingly clear message that looking to the market for economic protection and stability can be dicey indeed. The mindset of these reformists should send a chill up and down the spines of those who depend on a pension, social security, or both.

Also overlooked is the human nature factor in retirement planning. Simply put, too few exercise the necessary discipline to adequately prepare for life many years down the road. We receive mixed messages on literally a daily basis: live for today, don't worry about tomorrow, but as an aside you should plan for tomorrow. But how can we live for today to the fullest extent possible and not worry about tomorrow if we must save for tomorrow today? An interesting conundrum.

The fact is, there are people who need some form of authority that assures financial planning for the non-working years. Following the period of the Great Depression and the end of World War II, both private companies and government agencies, driven by the growth of labor unions, provided pension plans for their employees. But, as with any program designed to provide a needed benefit, pension programs were expanded beyond their original purpose of providing a safety net, and not a sole source of high living. Pensions for the higher-paid workers have reached unprecedented levels. Too many employees were engaging in what has been erroneously branded as double-dipping; that is, receiving a pension while employed and salaried by the same company or government from which they were drawing the pension. The fact that pensions are part of the employment contract and therefore not handouts is lost in the debate. (Similarly, employees pay part of their wages to the social security trust fund, so that when they start drawing these benefits, they are receiving funds from a source to which they contributed. This is hardly the stuff of a handout.)

I do not excuse labor from the pension problems. Earlier in our nation's history, during the administration of FDR and beyond, labor unions became so powerful that they were able to control much of the political climate, and their demands became increasingly excessive with each successful venture. Labor, therefore, is not blameless. But society, like a pendulum, swings back and forth, searching for balance. And eventually, a pendulum that swings too far left or right will begin swinging the opposite way. Political scientists call this dynamic a version of the Hegelian Dialect; that is, the existing system is the thesis, its opposition is the antithesis, the clash of the two results in the synthesis, which becomes the new thesis. Society can be likened to a pendulum, constantly swinging back and forth searching for balance.

Abuses in well-meaning, beneficial programs are certainly not new; throughout history, we have seen many such programs extended so far beyond their original purposes as to become unrecognizable. But rather than focus on the abuse, the tendency appears to be wholesale destruction of the program, using as the evidentiary basis the relatively small, but most glaring, examples of the abusive extension of that program. In short, the small worst-case example is viewed as the entire problem. This is nonsense; address the problem, not the entire program. To this end, we must direct our political leaders to shed the ideological babble and act like statesmen focusing solely on the public interest, rather than pandering to the emotions of their base with inflammatory, illogical rhetoric. This, however, in light of our current political climate, may be too much to ask for.

The excesses of the pension programs have become the focal point of resentment, to the point that we have reached today, where government officials want to end pensions, incredibly with the support of some who will be adversely affected should such a circumstance eventually ensue. The same may be said for social security; many who want to see it end or its effectiveness as a safety net reduced are those who will rue the day this happens. Perhaps they are not smart enough to realize this consequence.

I cringe when I hear legislators, as justification for their version of pension "reform," decry the status of state pension funds as not properly funded to meet future needs. (For Florida, the evidence is overwhelming that the state's pension fund is fully funded to meet future needs. There are legislators, however, who will not be dissuaded by the facts.) I recall that some states several years ago actually raided their respective public retirement funds to pay for other government functions. In short, any shortfall-- assuming the credibility of this claim--is at least in part a result of the raiding of these funds. For government officials to justify reducing or eliminating public service pensions because of the problem they helped create is not only the height of arrogance, it's absolutely false. If a private company did this, its officials would have to take their tail-between-their-legs argument to the judicial system.

What I find most incomprehensible is why so many middle class members support those who want to end pensions and reduce social security benefits. It is the middle class, or certainly a vast majority of the middle class, that is dependent upon, or will sooner rather than later become dependent upon, social security and pensions to survive economically. Perhaps they are caught up in the emotional wave caused by such an intense focus on examples of abuse, that they can't see--or refuse to see--the forest through the trees.

If these two economic safety nets are to be truly reformed so as to provide the maximum protection in the most efficient manner possible, our elected representatives should be compelled to reform them so that they remain actual viable safety nets; throwing out the baby with the bathwater--eliminating pensions and reducing social security benefits, the latter which are presently capped at less than $30,000 a year--is a prescription for disaster.

Perhaps one way to reduce or eliminate the abuse in public and private pensions is to place a cap on them, as has been done with social security. With the higher pensions going to those who earned the higher incomes, the purpose of pensions--to provide a solid but limited safety net--has been lost to regarding pensions as necessary to fund a higher lifestyle to which these highly-paid officers and employees have grown accustomed. This shouldn't be, particularly since the more affluent have most likely accumulated a nice nest egg for themselves through prudent investments, even during economic downturns.

It should be obvious that any shift from pensions to dependence on the stock market for retirement income is, as 2008 most recently demonstrates, fraught with peril.

As a personal note, many blame term limits for state legislators, resulting in the election of single-issue candidates, as a reason that the Republican-controlled Florida legislature is hell-bent on eliminating pensions. The state constitution limits House members to four consecutive terms; senators are limited to two four-year terms. Clever GOP gerrymandering of legislative districts since 1992 has no doubt contributed to the election of an ideological early 20th century mentality that now controls not only the state legislature, but Florida's congressional delegation as well.

Gerrymandering by a political party that favors incumbents and the party in power is certainly nothing new; the Democrats did this quite well up to the end of the 1990s.

But term limits is another matter altogether. Certainly, limiting legislators' terms affects institutional knowledge and, when combined with single-member districts, can easily lead to the election of single-issue candidates with little knowledge or appreciation of the many varied and nuanced issues that confront the state.

In the late 1990s, a lawsuit was filed challenging the amendment to the Florida constitution that provided for term limits. The argument was made that if the voters wanted to limit a legislator's term, all they had to do is vote him or her out of office. While the term limits amendment was upheld by the Supreme Court, I felt that this amendment was a mistake, because what would be sacrificed is the institutional knowledge necessary to protect against the passage of what history tells us is bad legislation. I firmly believe that those who fail to learn the lessons of history are condemned to repeat them. As for throwing out bad legislators, look to the most recent mid-term elections, where although the popularity of Congress was at an all-time low, only two incumbents lost their House seats. Incumbency is a powerful tool; it seems that however much the voters dislike Congress, they don't extend their dislike to their own congressman or congresswoman.

We are seeing the very real possibility of repeating what I thought we learned from the Great Depression and its aftermath. I hope I am wrong.

Oh, did I mention that I was the lead attorney for the state in the defense of the term limits amendment? I won that case; I wish I hadn't.

I think that the circumstances of my wife's and my retirement income is what was initially contemplated by both pensions and social security. Our pensions alone would not permit us to live a lifestyle similar to the one we enjoyed while working. The same can be said for our social security income. But both together allow us to enjoy such a lifestyle, with some minimal alterations. This should be the case for all retirees who receive a pension and social security.

Another critical aspect in financial planning for retirement is that we have no debt. No mortgage. No car payments. No loans.

No credit card debt that can't be paid in full each month. Debt is the greatest barrier to economic security in retirement. But being debt free takes commitment, perseverance, planning and--most important of all--discipline. I wish others exercised the necessary discipline.

Those who take the time early on to discipline themselves in part by dealing with debt will avoid much of the worry associated with financial planning for retirement. No one will do it for them. I am thankful my two daughters and sons-in-law have learned these important lessons. I know they will pass them along to their children.

One of the policies that purportedly addressed economic inequality beginning in the late 1960s was affirmative action. In an effort to make up for past racial discrimination, plans were instituted, predominantly in education and the workforce, to give blacks points or credits not available to anyone else. Admissions to college; job preferences; you are most likely familiar with these efforts. The courts struggled mightily with them when claims of reverse discrimination reached the judiciary.

I think that, intellectually, Democrats and liberals support affirmative action, at least until it hits home. This happened twice to me.

The first time was in the early 1970s. The dean of the law school from which I graduated convinced me to leave my job and return to my alma mater as assistant dean for alumni affairs, and teach courses on professional responsibility and mass communications law. I was exhilarated at the prospect of returning to law school as a faculty member. Less than a month after joining the faculty, however, I received a form letter from the dean advising that my position was affirmative action-impacted and that he couldn't assure me of a continuing contract beyond that academic year. He never mentioned this during the entire hiring process; not during the time he encouraged me to apply, not during the interview, and not after I was hired.

I had given up a fairly good job; Harriet and I had our first child on the way, and the dean--the one whose name appears on my law degree--never told me that this job was potentially a temporary one-year appointment. I was furious. I told him my situation, but he didn't appear sympathetic and simply shrugged his shoulders.

I continued to honor my contract and fully performed my obligations as assistant dean and instructor, all the while searching for another job. Finally, after several months of searching, a friend informed me of an opening at a state agency. She, also an attorney, told me she already put in a good word with the general counsel. I met with the agency's top lawyer, and was offered a position as staff attorney, at a salary about $2,000 a year lower than the one at the law school. Nevertheless, with a baby on the way, and bills to be paid, I eagerly took the job.

When I told the dean, he was upset that I was leaving even before it was finally established that affirmative action would kick in and preclude my re-appointment. He said I wasn't honoring my contract, which had about three months left. I was mortified at his reaction. I made it clear that he put me in this difficult position, that I had to provide for my family, and that I was leaving at the end of that semester and not returning for the last one.

We didn't speak for many years thereafter, and every time the law school hit me up for money during its annual fundraising effort, I made it clear that after what my alma mater did to me, I wasn't going to give the school a cent. Finally, long after the dean retired and another dean took over, I relented and began making an annual donation. But I made it clear that my donation was to be used exclusively for library purchases, and not for anything having to do with affirmative action.

The second experience took place in 1997. I had been a lawyer for 27 years, had a sterling reputation, had argued cases before both the United States Supreme Court and the Florida Supreme Court, as well as other federal and state courts throughout the south, and had held several offices with the state and local bar.

A vacancy occurred on the Leon County Court bench, and in accordance with the state constitution, at the time of a vacancy, the particular judicial nominating commission that makes recommendations to the governor for appointment, sets a time frame in which to submit applications, and then sets a schedule for interviews. I timely submitted an application, along with letters of recommendation--including one from my boss,

Attorney General Bob Butterworth--and received what was obviously a form letter acknowledging receipt. The submission deadline came and went, and I heard nothing further.

Then, one day I happened to meet an acquaintance who had also applied, and he told me "the fix was in." I asked what he meant, and he said that the appointment was going to go to an African-American applicant who had less than half of the number of years of Bar membership that I had, and whose employment was largely administrative in nature and not the kind of litigation experience of which I had an abundance. Shortly thereafter, I received another form letter noting that there were many qualified applicants and that the choice was a most difficult one, but a choice was made; however, the commission encouraged me to continue to apply for future openings.

Months later, I ran into a member of the nominating commission, a lawyer whom I knew for quite some time. I asked him about the process, and why I never even received an invitation to be interviewed. He hemmed and hawed; repeating what was in the form letter. I picked up the unmistakable message and moved on. I never applied for another vacancy.

Many of these affirmative action efforts are steeped in efforts to level the economic playing field. If this is to be accomplished, however, it will take education, discipline and a commitment to succeed. Today, there are no barriers to attending school, getting an education, and getting the necessary credentials to be competitive in the workforce. As I mention a bit later, we are a society of mixed values, which adversely affect the belief in the absolute need for an education in order to have any chance to succeed in life.

Before moving on, there are two quotes that seem most proper in globally addressing economic inequality. For the wealthy: to whom much is given, much is expected. For the downtrodden: God helps those who help themselves. Problems that cut across all societal lines are not solved by one group alone; it takes a concerted effort for all involved to commit to do their best if the American dream is to be attainable by all. To this end, each person must ask and honestly answer this ultimate question: am I doing the best I can to contribute to the greater good of society?

4. "The only thing we have to fear..."

Several years ago, former senator and 1972 Democratic presidential candidate George McGovern visited Tallahassee for a speech and book-signing. During his remarks, he noted with great concern how the Republican Party has, over the years, used fear to accomplish its electoral goals. He was most prescient in his speech.

Fear will paralyze; if enough people are scared often enough, those who instill it will reap their rewards. We saw this most recently in the 2014 mid-term elections, where it seems all a GOP candidate had to do was utter three words to instill fear and secure victory at the polls: Obamacare, liberal and Pelosi. I don't recall any Democrat uttering Boehner, McConnell or conservative to evoke fear. The reason for this is obvious: they don't resonate, simply because the Republicans have been far more successful in engendering fear through their sound bites and buzzwords.

Here is a classic example. The GOP demonizes Obamacare; the House of Representatives voted dozens of times to repeal it, knowing that such action was a waste of time because it would go nowhere, especially with a Democratic president. Yet, instead of dealing with people issues like immigration and the environment, those elected representatives wasted time and money solely to appease an ideological base. Then, when the Democrats call them out, the GOP calls them arrogant. Talk about the pot calling the kettle!!

These are the same people who, rather than deal with issues of general public importance, continue to adamantly believe that, with a global population of more than seven billion and millions of motor vehicles and businesses spewing noxious fumes, there is no such thing as man-made climate change, or global warming. These folks believe that humans are not a factor in any adverse environmental condition. Think of this; the fact that several billions of people and millions upon millions of motor vehicles and businesses spewing pollutants in the air daily has absolutely no impact on our environment! Not even a smidgeon. If all the people, vehicles and businesses were removed from the Earth, the environment would be just as it is today. What an incredible position to take; yet, they and their supporters march in lock-step to this mantra.

These folks point to frigid winter weather in the north as evidence that global warming is a myth. Never mind the melting glaciers, rising coast lines, draughts when and where there should be rain, weather patterns that defy precedent, and on and on. These people want facts; they want to see clear evidence of man-made global warming before they accept this as fact, or so they say. It is impossible, however, to see facts when their heads are in the ground like ostriches and refuse to see the undeniable scientific evidence that tells the story.

Yet, when it comes to facts that support evolution, they don't want facts; they are content to rely purely on faith. Why don't those whose faith allows them to deny evolution use the same faith to at least concede that there might just be something to global warming? Why can't they proceed in an abundance of caution just in case they might not be exactly 100 percent correct that global warming is a myth? These right wingers accuse the left of being arrogant; yet, are they not equally--or even more--arrogant in ignoring clear scientific evidence of man-made global warming and steadfastly clinging to their anti-climate change mindset? They are quick to tell others how to live--prohibit abortion for others; prayer in schools and other public places in which there is a captive audience; carry guns in schools and public places that potentially put others at risk; and on and on. And yet it is the Tea Party types who have the effrontery to accuse the left of being arrogant.

Perhaps the answer is determined by who benefits by denying global warming. Certainly not the general public, whose health is adversely affected by noxious emissions. Those who benefit are the business interests; the oil and gas companies that make the products used to run our vehicles, and fuel and energy-producing businesses, among others. You don't think so? Where is the legislative push for solar or wind power so that we might place a lesser reliance on fossil fuels? I don't see it either.

Simply put, the global warming opponents are those who benefit economically by their steadfast position. By the time they get the facts that they say they need, it will be too late. But why should they worry? They won't be here.

Then we have righteous indignation over scandals involving IRS, NSA and FBI surveillance of private citizens without their knowledge or consent. These revelations recall two historical facts: (1) government lying is nothing new; and (2) government lying knows no particular political party or persuasion.

Government spokespersons assure us that evil has been, and will continue to be, unearthed, and everything done in the name of national security is legal and necessary. In other words, the end justifies the means. While convincing the public that all this surveillance is done in our best interests, officials, in an effort to destroy the messenger in hopes of preserving the message, demonize the messenger as a "rogue," "traitor" or "disgruntled" employee who simply cannot be trusted.

Rather than dealing with the root causes of such aberrant conduct--a belief that the laws apply to others and not to them, or that we should blindly trust them because they know what's best for us--blame becomes a finger-pointing contest, as if one side of the finger-pointers in government has clean hands and the other doesn't. The fact is neither side is lily white.

It's not that government lying and scandals will someday magically disappear; human nature doesn't work that way. The real question is whether we are willing to make the effort to do more than blindly accept the so-called official version of the truth; that is, are we willing to conduct a self-generated in-depth inquiry, examining as many sources as possible, and independently satisfying ourselves as to the veracity of what we're being told? We don't need spin, we need honesty. We can handle the truth.

In the absence of this self-generated inquiry, we can expect that some of our government leaders will take to the equivalent of the soapbox and preach fear and doubt, while castigating others even as they fail to offer anything of a positive nature.

What the fear monger overlooks, however, is that fear accomplishes nothing. Those who are cognizant of recent history remember that the Vietnam war was based on the notion from previous wars that "if we don't fight them over there, we'll have to fight them here." We know from the revelations in the Pentagon Papers that, not only was this false, but the administration knew that that war was unwinnable even as more than 50,000 gave their lives in this ill-gotten effort. Incredibly, the same argument was made to convince doubters to wage war in Iraq. No weapons of mass destruction--the linchpin mantra in support of that war--were ever found; the claims made in support of that effort were never substantiated. Yes, it's true, those who fail to learn the lessons of history are indeed condemned to repeat them.

Fear can be overcome only through education and a thoughtful discussion on policies that actually deal with problems and help people; this is what government and governing is all about. It's not about sound bites, ideologically driven emotions, or blind labeling that dumb-down the nuances of important issues.

5. Without meaningful education, we are doomed; mixed values

There are numerous books and articles in the public domain dealing with the notion that our political system is rigged in favor of the wealthy, the result of a culture war more than 50 years in the making. The best way to deal with any fear mongering that gives life to this culture war is, as I note previously, through an educated citizenry.

By education, I don't mean reliance on computers to solve our problems or answer our questions. I mean an effective education system from elementary through post-high school that teaches how to search and inquire; how to think. A quality education is one, by graphic example, that teaches the difference between "their," "there" and "they're." A system that teaches that the Internet is not knowledge; that Wikipedia is not the be-all and end-all source of information. The examples are numerous. As I point out in more detail in the section on technology, education must inform of the delicate balance between technology as a workable tool, and technology as the sole source for learning. We must focus on the former, and ditch the latter.

A functional, quality education system requires educators who know how to teach; students prepared to learn from the first day of class; and a citizenry that is capable of holding those involved in the system accountable to those who are paying for it.

In short, to have the kind of education system that will educate those in whose hands the future lies will require all of us to assume responsibility to, in effect, fact-check what we are being told by those in whom we place our faith and trust.

Just go to any bookstore and look under "current events," or go online and type in "politics" and you find book after book and site after site excoriating politicians--both left and right--for contributing to the rise of Big Business, Big Oil, Big Banks, Big Pharma, etc., at the expense of the middle class. Without exception, every author or commentator believes that any chance of leveling the playing field requires an informed, educated and involved citizenry.

But here's the dirty little secret. As the need resonates for an intelligent electorate if we are to have even a fighting chance of dealing with the plight of the dwindling middle class--as well as those among us who are poor through no fault of their own--the cost of education continues to rise as the quality of the product continues to decline precipitously. In short, at a time when the need for an educated electorate is most vital, studies tell us the sad story of declining reading, math and science scores, along with an abysmal showing in history and civics. We must turn this around, or we will surely reach the point of no return. And the speed at which technology is advancing means there is no time to waste. Technology is advancing at breakneck geometrical speed, and society is experiencing cultural lag in addressing this rapid change.

Technology has advanced to such a state that there is a increasing dependency on high-tech tools to provide us with answers to our questions. Too many believe that if there is a problem, they can simply rely on a computer to find the solution. The concomitant attitude seems to be that all conduct must be governed solely by statutes, rules, regulations, etc.; that is, every conceivable act that embraces the human experience must be set out in written directives, leaving no room for uncertainty that necessitates debate, or so they believe.

The danger of this mindset is that it removes the human element from the thought processes. Sacrificed are common sense, sound judgment and reasoned thinking. By overdependence on machines, we are sacrificing on the altar of technology the thinking processes that separate us from lower forms of life. Technology must be a tool; if it ever becomes the master, the consequences to society and civilization should be self-evident. By way of example, even the so-called best and the brightest students, when called upon to identify their sources in support of a position or opinion, note Wikipedia far too often for this type of over-reliance on technology to be an isolated occurrence.

The last thing we need is a dumb-down citizenry, but the studies noted above, as against the continuing technology revolution, paint a bleak picture. We are on a slippery slope, and it will require two things to gain the upper hand: first, our government must stop posturing, pandering, pointing fingers and fighting an ideological battle and actually come together as Americans and do the people's business--pushed by a strong, smart and determined electorate--the business they were elected or appointed to do in the first place. And second, we must assure human superiority over technology. News of the ability to create robots that can think and have some level of emotional processing should send a chill down our spines because, precisely at a time when the need for a well-educated citizenry is at its greatest, we are witnessing its decline. The reversal of this trend should have already begun.

To have any chance to counter this, we need to get our values straight. We are a society of mixed values; we have no difficulty paying athletes, movie stars, etc., outrageously exorbitant salaries, while the scientist diligently pursuing a cure for cancer or Alzheimer's makes a comparatively paltry income.

I get it that all of us should earn as much as we can, and if there is an employer willing to pay someone $10 million a year to hit a baseball, catch a pass in the end zone, shoot a ball into a basket, or shoot a piece of vulcanized rubber into a net, then more power to him.

And I get it that sports and entertaining are forms of escapism, designed to make us forget, even for a short period of time, our daily trials and tribulations of putting a roof over our heads, paying our bills, and generally dealing with life's twists and turns.

But the message that these mixed values send is unmistakable. Why should an inner city youth worry about school when he can outrun, outhit, outpitch, out pass, out dunk, or out shoot anyone else in his neighborhood? African-Americans see athletes, particularly in the NBA and NFL, making incredible amounts of money and believe they can do likewise. They aren't told pointedly that the chances of making it in either league is infinitesimal at best.

They, and others as well, need to be have instilled in them most graphically, the absolute importance of education. A college degree is a sure way out of poverty; but this takes discipline and effort.

And it would be most beneficial if governments placed more emphasis on science, medicine, and related subjects rather than naming a state rodent or tree. (I know this may be an oversimplification, but I hope the point is made.)

Universities and colleges would do well to emphasize the learned disciplines rather than building new field houses, practice fields, arenas and stadiums.

It is probably over idealistic to think such a turnabout could occur; but it's better to try to address our societal value system now, than come to the stark revelation later that it's too late to get it right.

6. Judicial diversity

Efforts are under way in Florida, and elsewhere as well, to increase diversity in the judiciary. I applaud any and all efforts to increase participation by minorities in our government, and make them equal part of the American fabric. However, I take issue with the notion that diversity in the judiciary must be based solely on a comparison of the percentage of minorities on the bench to the overall percentage of minorities in the general electorate. In other words, the currently floating argument for judicial diversity is if a state's voting age population is 15 percent African American, it therefore follows that 15 percent of the judiciary must be African-American. This is not a proper basis for addressing judicial diversity today.

Although this notion, which the Florida Bar supports, was rejected by the courts more than 20 years ago, most people in Florida don't realize how close we came to materially changing how Florida elects its trial judges.

The 1992 redistricting cycle I discussed earlier led to two challenges to Florida's system of electing county and circuit judges. The trial judges are elected by the usual majority vote system within the particular jurisdiction; a vote system that is virtually universal in its application. The same groups that brought the redistricting litigation filed lawsuits in Tallahassee and Jacksonville, claiming the traditional majority vote requirements acted to dilute minority votes and prevent

African-Americans from electing judicial candidates of their choice, in violation of the Voting Rights Act.

The challenging lawyers used voting data that purported to show that white voters overwhelmingly voted for white candidates and by sheer numbers, black voters voting for black candidates could not elect candidates of their choice. They claimed entitlement to proportional representation in the judiciary, and offered, as a "remedy" to accomplish this a process that included having each voter given the same number of votes as there are candidates. In other words, if four candidates were running for a judgeship, each voter would be given four votes that could be given to one candidate or spread among the others. The reasoning was that if there were one black candidate, black voters could use all four votes for that one candidate, while the white voters would spread their votes among the other three, thereby giving the black candidate a better shot at winning.

The courts, when faced with this proportional representation argument and this supposed remedy, pointed out that Florida's eligibility requirements for judicial office significantly limited the number of qualified African-Americans for the state's judiciary at that time. Statistics showed that African-American lawyers who are members of the bar and had five years experience (the constitutional requirements for a trial judge), were only 2.5 to three percent of the total number of eligible attorneys. Thus, the court found that if 15 percent of the judiciary were to come from this smaller percentage of eligible African- American lawyers, then African-American attorneys would have greater success in obtaining judgeships than white attorneys. In making this finding, the judiciary concluded that reliance on comparisons between the racial composition of the general population with the racial composition of the local judiciary was illogical and contrary to law.

The important point here is that judicial diversity is not to be based on the percentage of minorities in the total population; rather, it must be based on the percentage of eligible minority attorneys. In this light, if the judiciary is to be reflective of the total population, then efforts must be directed toward increasing minority enrollment in our law schools, and a greater number of minorities must choose to enter the legal profession and then, once they reach the required number of years of Florida Bar membership, make themselves available for the judiciary. I don't believe it's a secret that there are very well qualified minorities who would make solid additions to the judiciary, but are doing extremely well in the private sector. Simply put, there are minorities who do not want to enter the judiciary because it is less lucrative than private practice. But that is their choice. In passing, this is the same choice made by all lawyers, regardless of race. If they can earn more in the private sector, why seek a judicial office?

In any event, when the number of eligible minorities reaches a percentage level roughly in proportion to the overall population, diversity will cease to be an issue, at least with regard to the judiciary.

7. The 50s and 60s

I am a child of the 50s and became an adult in the 60s. The 50s was the "feel good" era. World War II was over, and the Korean War was winding down. This was the Golden Age of Baseball, Rock and Roll, etc. The 60s started out with the election of a young, vibrant president, John Kennedy, following the oldest man ever to occupy the White House (at that time), Dwight Eisenhower. The contrast couldn't be greater.

Then, in 1963, Kennedy was assassinated, and the Vietnam War intensified, causing more and more young men to be drafted and sent off to fight. The mood in the country changed; from a "happy days are here again" mentality, there was--over a very short period of time--a cultural seismic shift. Now, the young were protesting war; flower children joined in the chorus for peace and understanding; the young were telling one another to live for today and not worry about tomorrow; the Greatest Generation was taken aback at what they viewed as the scofflaw behavior of the young. The generation gap could not have been wider.

In the midst of this societal shift, I was about to graduate from the University of Florida and received my draft number from the United States Army. These numbers were selected randomly by date of birth. July 12 got number 22. With so low a number, there was no doubt I was going to be drafted sometime shortly after graduation in 1965. I tried enlisting in the Coast Guard in Miami Beach, which was then my home city. However, during the physical, it was found that I had a hernia. I verified this with my family physician. Shortly before that doctor visit, I received a notice from the draft board to report to the Army's Coral Gables office for examination, and to bring any notes from doctors regarding any medical issues. I asked my doctor, who had treated me for childhood asthma, to give me a letter, which he did.

At the draft board, all who were called were asked to present letters from physicians. I did so, and when examined, the Army confirmed the hernia. Thus, my medical status was a history of asthma, and a hernia.

A couple of weeks later, I received my classification from the Army: 4F; permanently ineligible for military service for medical reasons due to a history of asthma. Three weeks later, I had the hernia repair surgery. I figured if the Army didn't want me, who was I to disagree. Although I would have served in the military, I wanted it to be on my terms. Things have a way of working out for the best, however.

A few years ago, Florida State University did a series of shows tracing the university's history. Of particular interest was the 1960s campus turmoil, of which FSU was not spared. I was editor of the student newspaper during the late 60s and witnessed first-hand the type of campus turmoil that hit so many colleges and universities at that time. Thankfully, FSU was spared the violence, but there were demonstrations and sit-ins. I was asked if I could attribute the student unrest at the time to a single cause, what would that be. I didn't hesitate and gave him a two-word answer: the draft. This brought home to those of draft-age the personalization of Vietnam and the risk of dying in a war the reasons for which the young didn't understand. And, as we found out later, this war was not only not being fought to victory, but declared unwinnable. In short, our political leaders lied to a whole generation of draft-age youths.

I digress here because too many who fought in Vietnam returned home, only to be ostracized because of their involvement in an unpopular war that tore at the fabric of our country 50 years ago. They--mostly draftees--fought because our government told them to; it was our government that created the nobility of this effort that led these men and women to believe in the propriety of what they were doing. It's not their fault that they believed their government; they should be accorded all the respect and honor given to our fighting forces throughout history.

During this interview, I said the only difference between Vietnam and the middle east today is the draft. If we had a draft in the 1990s or today, you would see demonstrations as we did back in the 60s. Why? Because human nature doesn't change. For World Wars I and II, we had an identifiable threat; nations out to destroy us and our allies. We could point to Germany, Italy and Japan as the enemy. We truly believed, and justifiably so, that we had to fight them over there, or we would surely have to fight them over here.

This argument lost its impact in Vietnam, and when used again to justify war in the middle east, it was met with scant acceptance. If, in the midst of the Iraq war, the draft were instituted, you can bet you would see a repeat of the 60s. When I said this, the interviewer was skeptical, as were some of those who saw the broadcast.

But far more told me privately that I was absolutely correct. Just as the young back then didn't want to be drafted to fight a war in the jungle, so it is that today's young would not want to be drafted to fight a war in the desert.

I don't know if anyone has ever written a history comparing the 20s with the 50s and 60s. There are some similarities. The 20s was a time of social revolution; that's the main reason this period was called the Roaring 20s. War had given way to prosperity; women were given the right to vote; it was the time of illegal gambling and the speakeasy as alcohol was prohibited yet consumed mightily. People were living for today, not giving a care to the economic disaster that was just a few years down the road.

The 50s and 60s saw the "feel good" era morph into social revolution. War had given way to prosperity; the right to vote was extended to 18-year-olds; people were living for today, and not worrying about tomorrow.

Cultural shifts in both periods were found in music, art and literature. George Harrison, one of the Beatles, said in a TV interview that much of the Beatles music was influenced by the arrangements in notes and chords of some of the great lyricists of the 20s and into the 30s and even 40s, like Hoagy Carmichael.

So, is there a connection between these two dynamic eras in our nation's history? I think an argument can be made for such a view. After all, history does repeat itself.

The hard question is why we have war. There is, to me, a simple reason; one steeped in human nature. Every war ever fought--whether for power, religion, etc.--was founded on an "I'm better than you" world view. There are those fanatics who believe their religion, and theirs alone, possesses the true word of God and, therefore, other religions--as well as those who have a different view of their own religion--are inferior and therefore infidels or vicars of evil. One race thinks it's pure, therefore, others are inferior, and must be cleansed. And on and on. The penultimate fact is that we're all short-term residents on this one planet; we are all part of one human race; all part of one world civilization. We must strive to live and work together, or we will surely perish by our own hand.

8. Law enforcement and the community

I begin this section with a disclaimer. One of my sons-in-law is a former law enforcement officer; the other is. Over the past couple of years, law enforcement has come under attack because of a few instances in which white officers shot unarmed black youths to death.

Black leaders joined with protesters, claiming racial profiling and emphasizing that the youths were unarmed. A further claim made by these leaders and protesters is that these youths were merely innocent young men just doing what youths will do, and not causing any problems.

Not a single law enforcement officer was ever criminally charged, and in the most flashpoint cases, the United States Justice Department, headed by an African-American, found insufficient evidence to press charges.

It is a sad day when a young man loses his life as the result of a violent act. But using the mantra of "police brutality" as the cause of black men losing their lives creates a scapegoat that overlooks the failure to address the root causes; and they are numerous and complex.

Whether we choose to admit it or not, and whether we like it or not, law enforcement is the last line of defense to anarchy. Those who choose a career in law enforcement are supposed to enforce the law without fear or favor. The law is what legislative bodies pass; it is not the law officer's job to determine what the law is, or to enforce it differently depending on the situation or people involved.

Are there law enforcement officers who use their badge to intimate and harass, and engage in taunting and abusive conduct? Of course. And they should be held accountable and weeded out of the profession. Are there those who use law enforcement as an excuse for their economic and social plight, and believe that their woes are fully attributable to police brutality? Of course. And they should be pointed out and held accountable as well.

What is common about these flashpoint incidents is that, in all cases, the deceased was portrayed initially as an innocent youth. Ultimately, the facts showed--and the judicial system concluded--that the officers involved reasonably feared for their lives, were assaulted by these youths and acted in self-defense as this term is defined by law.

The media (and I don't include social media because I don't consider that form of information exchange to be journalism) showed pictures of the youths as they appeared years earlier; they didn't show pictures of them contemporaneous to the time of the several incidences. All were significantly taller and/ or heavier than the officers involved. There was scant or no mention of drugs or alcohol as possibly contributing to the youths' behavior. Those who deny those facts that cut against the claim of youthful innocence and in support of the rallying cry of "police brutality" are actually enabling those who blame others rather than taking an introspective look at themselves.

Being a former newspaper reporter, I understand the drive for getting a sensational story before the competition. But reporters are schooled (at least, they used to be) in getting the story right. It shouldn't take a trial for the press to finally report all relevant facts that they had at the time of, or shortly after, the incident; that's the reporter's professional obligation. Get the full story, and get it right. Then report it without bias.

From my perspective as a former journalist, I have to ask myself whether the media truly understand and appreciate the role they play in fanning the flames of racial tensions; whether they see themselves as contributing to the racial divide by their one-sided reporting. And if they do, do they care? Do they truly engage in introspection and ask whether they are contributing to the problem by the manner in which they report these conflicts?

Let me use one graphic example. In this incident, one person claimed to see the youth--well over six feet tall and over 275 pounds--with his hands raised, and this supposed eye witness is heard uttering "hands up, don't shoot" which was attributed to the youth. This video went viral, and the mantra among the blacks was "hands up, don't shoot." This aired for several days before the actual facts began to emerge. This youth was shown robbing a store; the forensic report showed that the fatal wound was to the top of this youth's head; the officer who fired the fatal shot after firing several non-fatal shots claimed the youth attacked him while the officer was sitting in his vehicle; he sustained facial injuries that required treatment.

This officer was cleared by the local grand jury and the United States Department of Justice. Why? Because the physical evidence supported the officer's version that he was in reasonable fear for his life. The key question, which the media should have addressed at the outset, was how could a young man that tall suffer a fatal wound to the top of his head if he were truly raising his hands in surrender and saying "hands up, don't shoot?" Remember, the officer was shorter and was sitting in his vehicle at the time of the shooting. The "hands up, don't shoot" chant was vividly drummed home by the protesters and became a catchphrase that enabled them to--in their own minds-- justify destruction of property and threats and assaults on law enforcement officers.

When the spokespersons for this youth appeared on TV, they were curiously not pressed on the physical evidence. When finally asked about the trajectory of the fatal shot, they leveled accusations of character assassination. What was missing was the answer to the question. Was this a media accountability failure? Were the media not interested in getting these spokespersons for the victim to finally admit to a fact that ran counter to the mindset that the press had helped create?

The media's responsibility is to report all the facts; this is what balanced and fair reporting is all about. The failure to do so in a socially responsible way in these types of situations results in the promotion of racial tensions.

Several months after this incident, during yet another protest of this shooting, a black man shot two white police officers. While the first shooting received wide and continuous media coverage, the shooting of two white police officers received relatively scant coverage. Why? Where were the black community leaders calling for condemnation of such actions? The media are quick to report the protests, and the violence that ensues. Where are they when white officers are assaulted by black perpetrators?

There are several bloggers who were posting comments instigating violence against police officers. Why aren't these bloggers exposed for the hate-peddlers they are? And where is the black leadership joining forces to universally condemn such behavior?

The media and protesters' emphasis in these instances is on the youths being unarmed, as if our laws permit youths to do as they wish in threatening, taunting and assaulting police officers and not risk suffering ultimate consequences solely because they are unarmed. I'm not aware that only an armed person can present a legitimate threat to an officer's life and limb. I would hope we never reach the point at which officers are legally obligated to determine without a doubt that a perpetrator is unarmed, and that the officer can never legally defend himself or herself unless the perpetrator is armed. This would lead to a mass exodus from the profession, among other things detrimental to society.

While some in the media print glaring headlines and show film of racial protests over white officers shooting black man, they are curiously silent when a black officer shoots a black man, or when a white officer shoots a white man. I suppose their view is that race shouldn't matter, but all too often, their manner of coverage speaks volumes to the contrary. Those in the media who pander rather than report need to examine in great detail whether they are operating in the mode of the great reporters, like Edward R. Murrow and Walter Cronkite. That's the model the media should be following, rather than those whose rants and blogs on social media turn fiction into fact and call for a war on law enforcement officers.

Those who blame all law enforcement for the actions of a very few are just as racist and bigoted as those who blame all blacks for being thugs and criminals based on the actions of a very few. The point is that isms are silly and counterproductive. In the last analysis, it doesn't matter if someone is black or white, Hispanic or not, male or female, multicultural or not, gay or not, etc. What matters is how a person acts. Martin Luther King had it right; what matters is content of character.

It behooves law enforcement to make certain that officers who are in the line of duty and at peril of being in harm's way are sufficiently trained and free from any intent of abusing the badge by unlawful force or intimidation. And it behooves the black communities that are served by law enforcement to teach the youths not to taunt, challenge, threaten or assault law officers. It needs to be made abundantly clear that anyone who assaults an officer, whether armed or not, is putting his life in jeopardy. No officer is required to determine whether the youth has a weapon or not before defending himself; the officer who is imminently threatened with attack, or under attack, will not choose to err on the side of no weapon. He or she will defend with deadly force if necessary.

By way of summary, those who would drive a wedge between law enforcement and "the community" are doing a disservice to both. Law enforcement is a vital part of the community; they should be in partnership, pursuing the same goal: a safe and secure community. All efforts must be made to bridge any gap; demonization is destructive of community.

In section 3, I focused on economic issues. At its heart, the issues pertaining to race are economic in nature; this is what we as a nation should be focusing on. How do we empower those who are poor to lift themselves up? If they show initiative, shouldn't government be there to assist? If they don't, are there ways to motivate and encourage steps to be taken to achieve upward mobility? These are questions that go to the heart of our society; questions that seem to be lost as the wealthy strive to gain more wealth while the middle and lower classes are faced with growing adversity.

I believe much of the putative racial divide is born of the "I'm better than you" mentality that I mentioned earlier as a driving force behind war. If everyone were of the same color or nationality, there would be no racial or ethnic divide because we would all look alike. But while we are all created equal, we don't look or act alike. It's this cultural difference, however, that is our richness; this cultural wealth is what we should be focusing on, rather than differences based solely on birth status.

As long as people are different, there will always be bigotry; hatred or animosity based on superiority (and that others are therefore inferior) knows no race, religion, ethnicity or sexual preference. The key to addressing bigotry is to expose it for what it is, and thereby allow common sense and human decency to prevail. Recall Martin Luther King's famous statement about content of one's character, not the color of one's skin.

As this societal debate is waged, there are some things that can be done in the short-term. For those predominantly black communities, it would behoove those in leadership positions to promote education and career training for the young, and help them get into school and get that diploma or degree; those who are in school must stay there and get that vital education. Perhaps they can get an education to become police officers. Those who are looking for work might seek employment with local law enforcement agencies, as these agencies simultaneously reach out and recruit qualified and dedicated men and women from the communities they serve. I hope we don't see a day when only black officers can patrol and safeguard black neighborhoods. This would be a sad day for our country, and send the wrong message to the rest of the civilized world.

Books have been written about the causes of social unrest and racial tensions, but unless and until the varied causes and solutions are actually addressed by those entrusted to address them, the tensions will continue, and the next incident will see a repeat of the finger-pointing and blame-casting that all too often follow tragic events such as those involving young black men and the police.

9. Technology's downside, and (for me) upside

This is another subject I wrote about in 2012, but my deep concerns persist because I don't believe we are making strides in properly balancing technological advancement with quality education necessary to produce tomorrow's effective leaders.

Several years ago, Andy Rooney, the late <u>60 Minutes</u> commentator, waxed eloquent on the importance of technology in making all of us better able to communicate with more people more rapidly. And yet, when asked whether technology made us a better people, he was unable to provide an answer.

Recently, I walked into a restaurant and noticed far too many people with buds in their ears listening to who-only-knows; couples sitting at tables texting away on their iPads and mobile phones, with little or no conversation--you get the picture. And I see this scenario playing out day after day after day in places of public accommodation.

With the world literally at our fingertips, millions and millions engage in social networking via Facebook, Twitter, etc., with more networks coming down the pike. We have bloggers, posters, etc., using a language that has no regard for correct spelling or proper grammar.

It is self-evident that technology is advancing at an accelerated pace. I remember when I used the latest model manual typewriter in high school. Carbon paper and mimeograph machines were state of the art. Research was done in libraries. In the last 40 years, technology has moved with lightning speed, advancing twice as fast in half the time. Machines are rarely if ever repaired; they are simply discarded in favor of the latest model, which will become obsolete sooner rather than later.

I fear that with all this technology advancing at breakneck speed, we are sacrificing literacy; we are losing the ability to communicate with one another on a face-to-face basis. Communications by word of mouth or by letter-writing are being relegated to history. Today's young are not being taught to read, write or compute by using their God-given brains. They harbor a belief that all answers lie in the computer, as if machines can doing all the thinking for us.

A computer, however, cannot teach common sense, good judgment, or sound reasoning. Logical thought is a human condition; it can't be assigned to a machine, and a machine can't replace human judgment. Yet, it seems we are moving in the direction of having computers actually doing the thinking for us.

This is a dangerous trend; it can't lead to anything that is beneficial to society. Certainly, computers have their place; they can provide valuable assistance. But they can't replace that vital, singular factor, the human factor; judgment, reason, logic, rational thought.

Let me give you a graphic example from several years ago just to make the point. Under law, the Donald L. Tucker Leon County

Civic Center in Tallahassee was required to enforce a policy of no underage drinking; certainly a well-meaning, common sense policy. However, in an effort to remove the judgment factor, all civic center personnel were instructed to examine each patron's identification card. One night, Harriet and I took her mother, then in her late 80s, to an event. She wanted a glass of wine. The waitress promptly asked her to produce her ID. Now, you can easily figure that people in their 80s look like they're over 21. I don't know a single person in their 80s who looks 21; not even the richest Hollywood starlet with multiple facelifts could pull this off. Yet, when this waitress was asked why my mother-in-law had to engage in such a folly, she simply said it was "policy." She was embarrassed, but my mother-in-law was thrilled that she had to produce her ID; this had never happened before.

Again, no judgment or thought was required; just look at the birthday on the ID. Of course, whether an ID is fake is a matter that probably didn't cross the mind of the person who set this ludicrous policy; so long as the judgment factor is removed, the wisdom of this policy is of no concern. This jettisoning of judgment appears to be becoming more and more common, to our collective detriment.

Unless we superintend the machines we're creating, we risk becoming enslaved by them. And no one has to tell you the dire consequences of surrendering our status as the masters of our fates, captains of our souls to a machine.

In the section on education, I discussed a precipitous decline in the system, and the product it's supposed to produce. Incredibly, instead of addressing this decline, it seems we are further institutionalizing it to the point of acceptability. Here's one graphic example. It should surprise no one that driving requires concentration; a keen awareness of traffic, traffic signals, etc., always alert for the unexpected. However, at a time when there should be a greater focus on reducing the potential for driver distraction, technology has added to it. Now, when drivers are behind the wheel, they have a host of options in addition to driving--all of which are distractions. A driver can talk on his cell phone, text, check his GPS; you get the point.

Add these distractions--and the number is growing--to a society plagued with a declining education system, and we wind up with a prescription for severe consequences. One simple solution is to ban use of these distractions while driving, with violators facing stiff penalties. If you don't think this is a particularly serious problem, pick a day when you're doing some significant driving around town, or on the highways, and keep tabs on those who are on their phones or sending text messages. On second thought, don't do this; this might only distract you. Have a passenger do this instead. Or have a relative or friend drive while you make note. You'll quickly see what I'm referring to.

I'm glad I lived to experience life in the 50s. This gives me--as well as others in my age group--an appreciation of what life was then as compared to now. We have seen more technological advancement in the last 60 years or so than in all the time preceding it. Recall that just 100 years ago, there was no radio or TV; 30 years ago, there were no personal computers, and social network was unheard of; I could go on and on with examples of the rapidity of technological growth. And this expansion is continuing along at a geometric, rather than arithmetical, pace; which means that we can expect a continuation of twice as much innovation in half the time.

We can debate whether this explosive advancement has made us a better people intellectually, and imbued us with greater wisdom. I do believe, however, that we have suffered one serious loss--one that is attributed to the mantra of political correctness but is one effect of this rapid technological growth. That loss is the ability to laugh at ourselves.

In the 50s, I was entertained by the Three Stooges, the Marx Brothers, the Ritz Brothers, Amos and Andy, Milton Berle, Sid Caesar, Dean Martin and Jerry Lewis, Abbott and Costello, Jackie Gleason, Red Skelton, etc. Variety shows that began with the dawn of television (and Ed Sullivan) lasted until Carol Burnett aired her last weekly show in the 70s. The types of creative comedic expression, built on the Golden Age of TV Comedy, allowed for pretty much everything--from pure physical slapstick to stand-up comedians--except vulgarity. Self-deprecating humor was viewed as just that--humor.

Now, for them to survive, sitcoms must have sexual innuendos; drama must have some form of violence or sexual overtones;

and music must have a similar edge. Movies that get a G or even a PG rating are generally not going to be as audience-driven as the PG-13 or R-rated pictures. I don't believe that relying on sexual innuendos for a laugh requires as much creative ingenuity as did TV's comedic golden age.

When Jimmy Carter was president, he talked about a malaise that affected the country's mood, and took much heat for it. That, along with Ronald Reagan's optimism, helped in Carter's defeat for re-election. Overlooked in that 1980 campaign was whether Carter had a point; that is, whether he was tapping into the notion that we were becoming a more dour, less humorous, people. What passed as legitimate humor back then will get a person fired today. The comedy that made millions laugh in the 50s wouldn't survive on TV today. This leaves me--and no doubt many others in my age group--with a certain wistfulness, a longing for a return to a time that is no more and will never be again.

All of this technology and the cultural shift that has occurred with it, must lead to some end point. What that point will look like, and when it will occur, will not be made known to my generation, or even perhaps that of my children, but everything has a beginning and an end. Why would the technological explosion and its concomitant societal changes be any different? It seems prudent to me to ask ourselves where this is going, and if we really want to go there.

There is one great upside to technology--at least for me--and that's the beneficial use of social networking, more specifically Facebook. The benefit is simple; I can see pictures and, even more enjoyable, videos of my grandchildren. Hailey playing her musical instrument or a picture of her beautiful face. Kelsie in her cheerleading outfit or a picture of her beautiful face. Avery just doing what an inquisitive child does; and her beautiful face. And Connor, just being two years old; and his handsome face. (If you think I'm bursting with pride as I write this, I plead absolutely guilty as charged.)

In today's rapidly paced world, a world in which too few take the time to write letters or send cards, it's refreshing and comforting to know that I can keep up with my family even though separated by several hundred miles. I thank my girls for taking the time to post on Facebook. Another plus about this particular social network is that I can play word games, and Amy, despite her busy schedule, plays games with both Harriet and me. This keeps my mind sharp. Perhaps that's one reason why she likes playing these games with me; she has a great sense of humor, and she might just consider this as a way for me to fight off senility.

10. Customer service, good or bad?

See if the following narrative appears familiar. You place a call to a business at, say, 8:30 a.m. and you get a recorded message that the business is currently closed, that business hours are nine to five, and that your call is very important to them and you should please call back during business hours. At 9 a.m., you make another call and either get the same recorded message, or you're on the receiving end of a busy signal. You try a third time shortly after 9 and get a recording that tells you all of their service representatives are currently assisting other customers, but (once again) your call is very important to them, so please stay on the line and your call will be answered in the order in which it was received. While on the line--and as a captive audience--you are forced to listen to a variety of advertising messages.

Familiar? Of course it is. There may be a variation here and there, such as getting the "service representatives are currently assisting other customers" at 9 a.m. sharp. You might ask: how is it that so many customers beat you to the punch as soon as the business opened?

The fact is, phone service technology has advanced to such an extent that phones can be programmed to switch from one recorded message to another at a fixed time, without any person intervening. Do these companies really believe that we believe that all of their service reps walked in the front door of the business at 9 and immediately got busy answering calls and assisting other customers? Company officials, particularly those responsible for customer service, need a wake-up call themselves; customers are not fooled by such a lame brush off via the recorded message.

Just once, I would like to have a recording that says something like this: "Hello. Some of our service representatives are currently (on a break, out to lunch, out sick or on vacation, or whatever else they might be doing). We don't have enough employees to handle the volume of calls (you will never hear a recorded message saying their volume is anything but high) and others are on a break or just being lazy and can't answer your call right now. You could wait, put your phone on speaker and keep it nearby while you do something more constructive, or you can call back (sure, and go through this scenario again). Whichever you choose, have a nice day." At least this if far more honest than the BS that we currently get.

Of course, on the chance that you might reach a live person on your first call, consider yourself fortunate, because it doesn't happen very often.

As for the unsolicited advertising, evidently phone ads work, or the companies wouldn't use them. I make a note to consciously commit not to purchase any product advertised when I'm trying to get competent, timely service on the phone.

Then there's the form letter acknowledging a customer complaint, but saying nothing about resolving it. Why companies waste postage and paper on such drivel escapes me. Here's the scenario. You are a customer of a company that provides a service. You contact that company by phone or email, and set out the nature of your concern. A few days later, you receive a letter, and it begins Dear First Name, Middle Initial and Last Name. Already your suspicion mounts; how often do you receive a letter that begins like this?

The letter thanks you for expressing your concerns and for your loyal membership. It then informs you that company management and appropriate supervisors review all "member concern(s)" to assist in improving services. The correspondence notes appreciation for your input and promises to address "concern(s) appropriately." The letter concludes by informing that if you have any questions, you can call a series of phone numbers.

I use quotes above because this is an actual letter I received from a company. Does the company believe that I'm fooled into believing this is a personal letter directed exclusively to me and addressing my particular concerns? I think the company believes precisely that, otherwise it wouldn't use a form letter such as this. And make no mistake about it, this is a form letter; it contains absolutely nothing of substance. The Dear First Name, etc.; the parenthetical pluralization of "concern" and the absence of any reference to my complaint or how it will be resolved are graphically telling. Its use is designed to assuage the customer into actually believing his or her concern or complaint is being resolved. The company most likely believes the passage of time will cause the matter to simply go away. And since the company uses such a form letter, it probably works precisely that way. This type of letter should be an insult to a consumer; but the company most likely believes the customer is too ignorant to figure out the import of this correspondence.

Not with me. Of course, I responded, noting that this is obviously a form letter, and that I want a definitive response to my "concern(s)" within a time frame fixed by me. Over the years, I have found that strong responsive letters generally have the intended effect. It is not necessary, or prudent for that matter, to be nasty; you get more with honey than with vinegar. Just let the facts--set out chronologically with no elaboration or emotion--tell the story in a firm and direct manner, and you will get positive results. The company will realize that one such letter can lead to another and another, with copies sent to better business bureaus, licensing agencies, etc. You get the message. And so did the company.

The important lesson is not to let companies believe they are so big and have so many bureaucratic layers that they can get away with treating customers like annoying afterthoughts. It is the customer who puts money in the business coffers and in employees' pockets; customers should never hesitate to remind companies of this. I assume you realize that all of this applies to government agencies and employees as well. You pay their salaries and are entitled to competent and timely service.

Finally, there is another aspect of consumerism that seems to impact retirees more especially. Evidently, businesses must have a particular soft spot for senior citizens. What other reason could these businesses have in calling the old folks every few days, or sending them correspondence daily?

Hardly a day goes by that I don't receive a phone call with a voice message letting me know that I'm eligible for a free cruise, or a new car, or whatever the company wants me to believe it's giving away. And thanks to those companies for providing me with daily mail; if it weren't for them, I would have no need for a mail box. I get family mail via email, and all bills are handled online. So, it's the good old junk mail that keeps Harriet and me running to the mailbox every afternoon.

And what wonderful mail we get!! Save social security (just send in a membership check); cut-rate cruises to anywhere in the world (providing I send in a deposit forthwith); a free inexpensive item, accompanied by a solicitation for a sizeable donation; the latest wonder supplement guaranteed to add years to my life for "only" whatever the amount is, with a discount if I act immediately; you get the picture. Even though I toss the junk into the garbage, the companies engage in this form of activity because they obviously have a successful rate of return. Go back to my section on education; the answer to "why do they do this" is there.

I think that when you reach retirement age, your name is given to just about every charitable and political organization so they can solicit you for money. They figure you have the money, and chances are you're home and will answer the call, or eagerly awaiting the mail.

On occasion, I will let it be known that my volunteer services are available, but evidently they're not interested in my service; it's my money they want. For example, when I get a letter from a political official I've never met, addressing me as "Dear George" and asking for a donation, I'm told that the "other side" is waging war on the middle class, or some other evil that's designed to get my attention--and my check. While technology allows for creating the impression that this is a personal letter from an official to me, I'm smart enough to know that's is a simple form letter. This type of letter obviously works, however, or they wouldn't use it. I hate to see money wasted on postage and paper, but that letter winds up in the circular file where it belongs. Besides, if they don't want my services, they're certainly not going to get my money.

The same is the case for charitable solicitations. I know which charities I want to support, and I do. Any other correspondence is a waste of paper and postage. It joins the other recyclable material.

I know what I'll do. The next time I get a charitable solicitation call, I'll engage the caller in protracted conversation, frustrating him because time is money, and then, when I've had enough, thank the caller and let him know that I need my shot of prune juice, and hang up.

11. Two other interesting cases I handled, and the unlevel judicial playing field

In my 2012 memoir, I wrote about some significant cases I handled over my 40-year career. I failed to mention two because they hadn't reached that level of significance at that time. They now have. The first gave me great personal comfort; the second didn't set any kind of precedent, but it was of note because of what the person involved did.

Spurred on by the deaths of young children by drowning in neighbors' pools, and alarmed that drowning is the second-leading cause of deaths of young children, the Florida Legislature in 2000 passed the Florida Residential Pool Safety Act, which set minimum safety requirements. Under this law, a pool must have at least one safety feature to pass final inspection and receive a certificate of completion. Safety feature options include fencing around the pool, an approved safety pool cover, or alarms on all doors and windows that have direct access to the pool.

Not all pool companies applauded this important safety measure, and a lawsuit was filed challenging the law as imposing Draconian and illegal burdens on these companies. The case was assigned to the Attorney General's office, and I was tasked to handle this lawsuit. I promptly contacted the sponsoring legislator, a young state senator from south Florida. She provided me with a voluminous amount of safety data and information regarding the number of tragedies that could have easily been avoided by installing the safety devices mentioned in the law.

After a heavily litigated case, the state prevailed, owing in great part to this legislator's dogged involvement in assisting me with the lawsuit. Now, anyone desirous of installing a residential pool in Florida must comply with this law. The sponsor of this legislation eventually moved on to become a congresswoman, and she was singularly instrumental in getting Congress to adopt a similar federal law.

Many years after the passage of the state law, this congresswoman appeared as the featured speaker at a club in which I am a charter member. During a question-and-answer session, she mentioned as one of her proudest accomplishments her work in getting this legislation passed. I was sitting at a table a few feet from the podium and during her speech, I could tell she was repeatedly glancing at me. When she finished her speech and asked for questions from the audience, I raised my hand, not to ask a question, but to thank her publicly for her assistance in the litigation, without which the outcome might not have been favorable. As I was speaking, I could see the look of recognition in her eyes. She made it a point to thank me for my efforts of more than 12 years earlier.

Her name is Congresswoman Debbie Wasserman Schultz, who as of this writing, is also the Chair of the Democratic National Committee.

Now, on to my second memorable case.

On I-75--or to be more precise, directly adjacent to this well-traveled interstate near Ocala--is a place known as Cafe Risque. It features nude dancers. Totally nude female dancers. And a full menu and beverage list. The company's large billboard advertisements, located on the highway, were the subject of an investigation by the Florida Department of Transportation, and the company was charged with having illegal outdoor advertising signs. Under Florida law, these signs must be of a certain size and distance from the roadway, among other requirements addressing highway beautification compliance. The owner of the company was cited for violating state law. It should have been an easy matter to remedy, but the owner, who faced constant harassment (his story) from local law enforcement authorities, wasn't going to take any guff from the state. So he decided to hire a lawyer and fight the citation.

I was called upon to represent the department, and proceeded to take the deposition of the owner. Evidently, he didn't like the questions I was asking, so shortly after I took his sworn testimony, he put up a billboard sign at the intersection of I-10 and I-95 branding certain people with the department--and me--as dummies, or words to that effect. I didn't know this when the sign was first posted; I found out when I began getting calls from those who knew me, drove on these heavily traveled interstate highways, and saw the sign.

Being curious, I drove the 100 miles from my home to this site, and sure enough there was my last name next to the last names of the agency administrators responsible for "harassment" of a "legitimate business owner." He kept the sign in place for several months, even after he lost the case at all levels. I saw it each time I drove to Gainesville to visit my daughter and her family.

Then, one day a few years ago, I read a story in the local newspaper that this owner--a relatively young man--had died suddenly of a heart attack. A few weeks later, as I was driving to Gainesville, I noticed that the sign had been removed.

An interesting story with a bittersweet ending.

The final part of this section pertains to the types of cases I handled during my time with the Florida Attorney General's Office; and during 24 years, I handled a lot of cases.

In school, we are taught that the law knows no distinction; all are treated alike. We are familiar with the scales of justice, the figure blindfolded, the scales equally balanced.

Whatever this symbol may mean in the real world, when the cases involve suits against government or government employees, those bringing these actions have a steep hill to climb. This is a result of doctrines and principles set out in constitutions and legislation, as well as those created by the judiciary.

While there are many types of claims that may be brought against the government, the two most frequently made are torts and civil rights cases.

Tort claims usually involve those of negligence against public employees. The Florida Constitution embraces the doctrine of sovereign immunity, meaning that the state and its officers and employees generally can't be sued for actions taken in their official, public capacities. However, Florida's constitution provides that sovereign immunity can be limited or eliminated by the legislature. In Florida, the legislature has limited the absolute bar of sovereign immunity to negligence claims only by prohibiting the naming or holding personally liable any officer, employee or agent, unless there is proof of bad faith, malicious purpose, or wanton or willful disregard of human rights, safety or property--an extremely hard-to-prove burden.

Further, while the state itself, as well as its agencies and subdivisions, are accountable for tort claims just like private individuals, damages are limited or capped at $200,000; any amount awarded in excess of this amount must be presented to the legislature as a claims bill for payment. At this point, the legislature is free to treat the matter just like any other bill--it must pass both houses and be acted upon by the governor.

Thus, the standard for negligence cases against the state is quite high; and the amount that can be obtained before the courts in a negligence action against the government is limited.

The other type of case--and the type I handled far more than any other--is the civil rights action under federal law. The key civil rights legislation provides that any person, acting under color of law, who deprives any person of the rights, privileges and immunities secured by law, may bring a legal action for damages to redress this conduct. Unlike state tort claims, a federal civil rights action for damages has no limit.

This short, relatively straight-forward paragraph, taking less than a page in the federal statutes, has over the years generated more litigation per statutory volume than just about any single piece of legislation. What does "under color of law" mean? What is a right, privilege or immunity that is secured by law? Added to these matters are the defenses that are uniquely available to judges, prosecutors, other public officials, employees and even witnesses who testify at trial--the defenses embraced by the doctrines of official and qualified immunity, and Eleventh Amendment immunity. These are immunities from being sued, regardless of the circumstances. Thus, no matter how egregious the conduct, if the immunity doctrine applies, there can be no lawsuit.

The rationale for these defenses for government and its officials is that, as the courts repeatedly say, public officials and employees must spend their time doing the people's work; they must not be permitted to devote their time and energies to wondering if their decisions and/or actions might lead to lawsuits against them by the disgruntled. They must devote all of their time focusing solely on what is required of them by their office or employ. Whether you believe this is a legal fiction, or legal mumbo jumbo, is of no force. And you are not asked to agree or disagree with this rationale; this is what the judiciary believes, and governs the reasoning behind these unique defenses to public sector lawsuits.

The Eleventh Amendment to the United States Constitution prohibits a citizen of a state from suing the state itself in federal court. The vagaries of the meaning of this amendment, determined on a case-by-case basis, take up quite a bit of space in the federal case reporter system. Books have been written on the impact of this amendment; for our purposes, just an understanding that this amendment poses a profound burden on anyone in Florida seeking to bring a civil rights action (or any action, for that matter) against the state itself is sufficient. So, if your name is John Jones and you want to sue the State of Florida in federal court, you have an immediate constitutional burden to address.

Official immunity from a civil rights suit extends to judges, prosecutors and others acting in these capacities; they can't be sued for actions taken in their official capacities, unless it can be shown that they acted in clear absence of jurisdiction or authority. For example, under the doctrine of absolute or judicial immunity, a judge can't be sued for erroneously signing an arrest warrant, even if the person committed no offense and, in fact, was wrongly identified. The remedy is to litigate the propriety and legality of the warrant, not a suit against the judge. A glaring example of a judge acting without authority is if, in the midst of a trial, he pulls out a gun and threatens those in the courtroom. Clearly, the judge is not acting like a judge in this instance. The cases are voluminous in describing the expanse of a judge's jurisdiction or authority for purposes of judicial immunity.

Prosecutors, in deciding to bring charges and prosecute a case, are absolutely immune from civil rights liability regardless of the circumstances or outcome. You might be familiar with instances where DNA evidence clears a felon many years after imprisonment. These cases rarely result in civil rights actions because the prosecutor's actions all occurred while prosecuting the case, and absolute or prosecutorial immunity applies in these cases. The cases setting out the parameters of this defense are equally voluminous.

There is an exception, however. Where the civil rights claim is directed to the investigation, rather than the prosecutorial decision and action, absolute immunity doesn't apply. Similarly, where absolute immunity doesn't apply under any circumstance, there is a lesser doctrine--one of equal force in precluding civil lawsuits--called qualified immunity.

Where absolute immunity is found to be inapplicable because of the nature of the official's actions, or where this form of immunity doesn't apply at all--instances involving all other officers and employees--qualified immunity will nevertheless bar a lawsuit.

The doctrine of qualified immunity protects public officials and employees from being sued for damages unless they violated "clearly established law" of which a reasonable person in his or her position would have known. This doctrine aims to protect civil servants from the fear of litigation in performing discretionary functions entrusted to them by law.

As the courts have repeatedly said, the qualified immunity test requires a two-part analysis: "(1) Was the law governing the person's conduct clearly established? (2) Under that law, could a reasonable person have believed the conduct was lawful?" Government officials and employees performing discretionary functions generally are shielded from liability for civil damages as long as their conduct does not violate clearly established statutory or constitutional rights of which a reasonable person would have known. The courts note that this doctrine protects all except the plainly incompetent or those who knowingly violate existing law.

What does "clearly established law" mean? And how is the court to determine from the facts whether a reasonable person in his or her position would have known existing law was clearly established, and that a reasonable person could have believed the conduct was lawful? The cases addressing these questions take up tens of thousands of pages in the case reporter system.

The above discussion on these defenses--which resulted in about 98 percent of my cases being dismissed--is not meant as an in-depth representation of applicable law. I hope you appreciate and understand how the law treats public officials and employees when they are sued for actions taken in the exercise of their respective office or employ.

There have been articles calling for the elimination of the absolute and qualified immunity doctrines, and of holding public officials and employees accountable just like non-public people. The danger in doing that is the timidity and fear that would accompany the decision-making of these persons; subjecting their actions to judicial second-guessing and after-the-fact back-seat driving. In balancing the scales, our jurisprudence sides with the public authorities, so that those who perform public functions can do so relatively free from worrying about potential consequences.

While there have been abusive acts committed by public officials and employees, the courts have opted to place these litigation barriers to protect them, rather than expose them to the vagaries of the judicial system. In the end, the decision to afford them this protection ultimately represents a value judgment by the courts.

12. Influential people in my life

Each of us has had people who have influenced our lives. Young boys and girls have their heroes, usually sports stars for boys, actresses or singers for girls. As a boy, I idolized Mickey Mantle, a great baseball player of the 50s. Only later did I find out that his life was not exactly the kind that justified such blind hero worshipping; toward the end of his life, even he recognized this.

As I got older, I came to the realization that sports heroes are human beings with the same failings and imperfections that are shared by the rest of us. I also realized that my heroes were those men who were with me day in and day out; my dad and grandpa. They were men who did an honest day's work for their pay. Their word was their bond. Their lessons were to be good to, and do right by, others. Simple, basic principles that should be a rule and guide for all of us. They provided verbal discipline when I deserved it. They never struck me; all they had to do to get me in line was to take away something they promised and that I really wanted, like going to a baseball game or movie. If I misbehaved, the game was off, as was the movie. It didn't take but a very few instances to convince me to get in line.

My paternal grandma was the most influential woman in my early years. She was a homemaker who, because of my parents' situation that I discussed in my memoir, was called upon in her 70s to help my dad when he moved to Florida after my parents' divorce, as well as help raise a 14-year-old (me) and a 10-year-old (my late brother) for three years.

My dad and his dad--grandpa--were the most influential men in my life. They taught me the important lessons of compassion, honesty, respect, the value of education--something neither one had--and how to live a decent life. They simply wanted me to have what they didn't have.

Of course, others have been influential in my life, particularly in my early career as a newspaper reporter and novice lawyer. I looked up to judges and senior lawyers who are too many to name here. They took me under their wings and helped me navigate the professional world. I hoped that as my career advanced, I was at least somewhat influential in helping a young student and lawyer along the pathway of life. This hope remains with me today.

In my adult years, the most influential people are Harriet and my two daughters. It is said that the child is the father to the man. Well, my girls have in so many ways been a parent to me. Although I never had a pet as a child, and foolishly thought that dogs were vicious and cats too independent, it wasn't until my children, particularly Amy, batted their eyes and gently persuaded me to have pets that I finally caved in. And as I wrote in 2012, their insistence made me a better man and father. Thanks girls, for all you did for me and all you had to put up with to get me to do what I should have figured how to do by myself, without your persuasive efforts.

I am so proud of the way Lani and Amy are raising their children. Their husbands, Brian and Frank, are both gentle and kind men who are raising their children with love and kindness, yet making certain that they are well-mannered and caring. Making intelligent decisions and being responsible for their behavior-- that's the message my children are giving theirs.

My grandchildren well know that a simple "please," "thank you" and "may I" go such a long way, and I have no doubt they will be successful because of the simple yet timeless rules that were instilled in me; that Harriet and I instilled in our girls even as my sons'-in-law parents were instilling these values in the men in my girls' lives, and they as parents are in turn passing down to my four grandchildren.

Although grandpa was what I was expected to be called, my oldest granddaughters, Hailey and Kelsie, dubbed me "grampy" when the oldest was five and her sister was three. My youngest granddaughter, Avery, picked this up, and I have little doubt her younger brother Connor will do likewise. So, grampy it is, and I love it when they ask for something with a "please" and a "may I" and conclude with a "thank you." Their parents stress this continually, and we know this will pay great dividends in the future. I only wish other parents were as concerned about and committed to good manners, good behavior and good decision-making as my daughters are. It makes this old guy very, very proud and happy.

I must digress here because, as I think about how my children were raised, and how fortunate I am to know how they're raising their children, I want to share with you a pet peeve; boorish conduct that I see far too often. When people are out in public, especially at a mall or restaurant, I think they want to enjoy the outing--especially if it's for just a few moments of peace and quiet that they are entitled to. So, the last thing they want to put up with are rude, ill-mannered, ill-behaved children whose parents are ignorant of or totally oblivious to their kids' conduct. Either that, or these parents will give you a silly smile and shrug it off as children just being children. They will make no effort to correct or control their kids' behavior, or hold them accountable for the scene they're creating. These parents show little or no embarrassment for such alarming behavior. To make matters worse, others who are equally put off by this scene usually shy away from making any comment for fear of retaliation by the ignorant or indifferent parents.

To these ignorant or indifferent parents I say, get your act together. Your children's behavior is neither funny nor "just kids being kids." Their behavior is exactly what we see: ill-mannered, inconsiderate, bad behavior that is a direct reflection on the parents, whether they want to admit this or not. Children need structure; they need discipline. If they don't get this at home, they won't have it in school, and they'll probably wind up being forced to get it in the penal system. I've seen too many brats in restaurants and malls--and other similar places--with the parents off in some other world.

We require licenses to drive, fish, hunt, etc. But we don't require a license to raise a child. While I certainly don't think a child-licensing system should be required, perhaps offering educational programs in child-rearing, with an emphasis on child behavioral development, would be a good idea. This course could be offered as part of a community's outreach service to those about to become parents. Perhaps I'm being idealistic in believing that those who most need such a course would participate, but if it enlightens even a few, it might just be worth it. There are folks out there who have children who don't have a clue how to raise them. Enough said.

Back to influential people in my life.

And the most influential is Harriet. I don't know how she put up with my impatience, occasional aloofness to family matters, and on and on, over so many years. She has the patience of Jobe, a great ability to laugh when I'm bouncing off the walls in one of my rants at some injustice...I could go on and on and devote a book just setting out examples of how she kept me in check for 44 years and counting, if I could remember all of them. A "thank you" here doesn't do justice to her influence in my life. She has been my life; I can't truly fathom my life without her.

She says we're traveling buddies now. We frequently pause and reflect on where the time has gone; it seems like yesterday that we met, dated, got married, had two girls, raised them, got them through college, met their special boyfriends who became their husbands, became grandparents four times, made it through professional careers, and now enjoy the fruits of our endeavors (some would call it labors, but there was nothing really laborious about the journey) in retirement.

Life is a journey; life is what happens when you're busy doing things. And Harriet and I have done so many things that have made this journey so exciting and challenging so far.

Finally, living in a state capitol, and working in and around state government, I have met many public officials who have helped in various ways to favorably impact my life. Without listing them all, I would like to note a few.

Claude Pepper was a United States senator during the FDR and Truman years, and served as a member of the United States House of Representatives from 1963 until his death in 1989. His 1962 campaign in Miami was the first local one I had ever been actively involved in. (I worked with other high school students in Miami Beach on John Kennedy's campaign for president in 1960.) I was Sen. Pepper's (everyone I knew called him Sen. Pepper) campus coordinator at Dade County Junior College. When I visited Washington, I made it a point to stop by his office just to say hello. He personally greeted me every time. Flash forward to the late 1980s. He had just published his memoir, and had a book signing in Tallahassee. I bought his book and, during the few minutes I had with him, showed him the letter he sent to me in 1962. He smiled and noted this in his book as he signed the cover page.

Years later, in 2000, I received the Claude Pepper award from the Florida Bar as outstanding government lawyer. And, along with Harriet, I joined the Osher Lifelong Learning Institute--OLLI--at Florida State University, headquarters located at the Claude Pepper Center on campus. I donated that 1962 letter from him to me thanking me for my work on his first House campaign to the Pepper Library and Museum archives.

I got to know and/or represented (in my service with the Attorney General's office) the following governors and attorneys general:

Governors: Reuben Askew, Bob Graham, Bob Martinez, Lawton Chiles, Charlie Crist and Jeb Bush. Attorneys General: Richard Ervin, Jim Smith, Bob Butterworth, Richard Doran, Charlie Crist and Bill McCollum.

Then there are the legislators, judges, state attorneys, mayors and commissioners (city and county), sheriffs, supervisors of elections, and lawyers--in particular my former law partners Steve Slepin and Paul Lambert, all of whom helped mold me as a professional, and as a man. Steve has been a confidante and advisor since the late 1960s. I am most grateful for his profound wisdom and brilliant intellect.

Through the years, people move into and out of our lives, but close friends will always be a part of one's memories. It has been said that if you can go through life and have a handful of good friends, you are indeed lucky. And by a good friend, I mean someone who, if the circumstances necessitated, you could call at 3 a.m. and that person would be at your home to do whatever you needed done. In this regard, I have been lucky indeed. So, to the best of my ability, here are close friends to whom I give thanks for being in my life then, and who are in my life now: Roger, Larry, Jimmy, Kenny, Raoul, Rick, Frank, Lenny, Dave, Chuck, Jim, Charles, Frank.

Thank you all, those who I have named, and those whose names I haven't listed. In my mind and in my heart, I know who you are.

13. College pranks

A few friends who read my earlier memoir commented that little was included about my undergraduate years in college. Harking to their days as students, they asked whether I did anything that, upon reflection, I wouldn't do today. My answer: sure, lots of things. Although they didn't say so outright, I know what they were looking for--mischief.

Now that so much time has passed; I can't be disciplined or otherwise held accountable for what I did; and in the interest of complete candor on my part, I recall a few pranks. Just a few.

Here is the first that I recall. I was a student at the University of Florida, living in a dorm with a psychology major whom I had met while attending Dade County Junior College in Miami. We agreed that, if we were both accepted to UF, we would room together.

We were assigned a room for two on the top floor of this dorm. There were four rooms on the floor, one next door to ours; the other two about 15 feet away across a small, narrow hall on the opposite side. Between each of the two-room sections was a common bathroom/shower and, on the opposite side, the stairway.

Early on, it was evident that the students assigned to the two rooms on the opposite side of mine, as well as our next door neighbors, were on the football team--as were some of the students on the floors below. What kind of students were they?

Loud, obnoxious, rude, bragging on being jocks...on their good days. Fortunately, they partied elsewhere on weekends, so my roommate and I were able to study then. During the week, however, it was a different story.

Since my roommate and I were considered eggheads, quiet and studious, we agreed no one would suspect us if we did a bit of payback for this loud, obnoxious behavior. Anticipating a long weekend break in a few weeks, we started saving newspapers, stacking them under our beds, in our tiny closets, etc. When our across-the-hall neighbors left for the weekend, my roommate and I began papering their room. For those unfamiliar with this prank, this is how it worked: you crumple each four-page section into a ball, open up the transom above the door, and toss wads of paper through the transom until the room is full. To open the transom, I lifted my roommate by cupping my hands and hoisting him up so he could push it open.

After we tossed as much paper as we could on a Saturday, we retreated to our room and, the following day, awaited their arrival. What made this prank workable is that the two in this room had a bit of a quarrel with their next door football-playing neighbors, so we didn't think we would be suspects. And we were right.

Sure enough, at about 10 p.m. on a Sunday, with the aid of streetlights, we saw the two jocks enter the dorm and walk up the stairs (the dorm had no elevator). We heard them mumbling as they neared their room. Our lights were off and we made no sounds. We visualized one putting his key in the lock and turning the doorknob. Then we heard the expletive-riddled wailing of two students. For days, the four jocks on that end of the hall squawked and squabbled at each other. They agreed that the prank must have been pulled off by the players on the lower floors....too many to actually finger. We were asked if we had noticed anything usual. Not us, we're just innocent students studying diligently trying to pass our classes, we told them. And they had no reason to disbelieve us.

But for the rest of the year, they caused us no further annoyance. I guess they were focusing too intensely on their peers below to bother with us.

The second prank was directed at our next-door neighbors. Although they weren't as obnoxious as the across-the-hall gang, they started becoming increasingly annoying. My roomie and I decided to pull the fire extinguisher gag. In the early 60s, fire extinguishers were large, cumbersome tanks that, under the fire code, had to be installed on each dorm floor. The one for our floor was directly opposite our room. When you turn these tanks upside down and press the lever, a flame-retardant foam is ejected through a rubber tube. Well, late at night, before turning in, my roommate and I took the fire extinguisher from it mooring, turned it upside down and leaned it against the door.

In the morning, we heard a loud commotion. Sure enough, when our neighbors opened the door to leave for class, the fire extinguisher hit the floor, compressing the lever, and setting off the foam that sprayed their room.

We weren't blamed because of our well-cultivated reputation as two nerdy geeks incapable of any such juvenile mischief. Once again, the footballers were our neighbor's target. Because this prank didn't lessen our neighbor's annoying behavior, my roomie and I concocted another scheme--the old matchstick in the lock routine.

Prank number three on my very short list is an easy one. You just take a wooden matchstick, stick it as far as possible in the lock, break it off and, using your key or a nail file, jam the stick as far as it will go. When the jocks got to their room and tried to go in, well, the yelling and screaming could be heard for miles. This is not a serious prank, because the dorm manager who lived two floors below had the necessary tools to disassemble the lock and remove the wood. Once again, players accused players; however, this time the prank worked, but only for a short time.

Their annoying behavior required my roomie and me to resort to the blazing door prank. This, too, is an easy one. Just pour some lighter fluid over the door, and strike a match. This caused the coating to bubble up, and made the doorknob quite warm to the touch. So, we observed our neighbors' comings and goings for several days for timing purposes. Then, one evening when they were out, we set the door ablaze. When they returned about 15 minutes later, we had our lights off and listened. The hallway was dark, so they didn't see the blistering, but whoever reached for the doorknob knew immediately what had happened.

My roomie and I pretended we were sleeping--it was about 10 at night--and that the commotion woke us up. Naturally, we were not suspects; our across-the-hall jocks took the full force of the blame. But good actually came from this prank; our next door neighbors ceased to be annoyances.

Our final prank was what we referred to as the waterfall episode. This one, however, was not our idea; it originated with our next door neighbors!! The loudest jock in the dorm was a huge fellow who must have had a hearing problem because we could actually understand what he was saying to his roommate and neighbors one floor below us. His normal conversation was at shouting level for the rest of us. Plus, he was obnoxious, as was his foul-mouthed roommate.

So, once again, with a long weekend break coming up during which most of the dorm would be vacated, now the four of us gathered newspapers and, when Friday came and the targets left, we waited for late in the day to take the papers into the shower, soak them in water, and shape them into a border, placed on both sides of the bathroom leading down the stairs and to the front door of the targets' room. Then, we went back upstairs, plugged up the drain, and turned on the shower. For just for a few minutes. We then proceeded to shut off the water, remove the plug, gather up the soggy border, mop up the floor and deposit the evidence in the trash container located behind the dorm.

You will have to imagine what their reaction was when they returned to their room Sunday night. Fortunately, only good things came of this; they ceased being a problem for all concerned, and nothing was left on their floor that might have been damaged by water.

Other than these minor pranks, I was a model student. Even if I say so myself.

14. My love of hockey

Now, you may ask, why does hockey get such a prominent place in this mini-memoir. Well, I will tell you. As a child growing up in New York City, I went to many hockey games involving the New York Rangers. My dad managed a hotel where National Hockey League visiting teams would stay, and he would frequently get tickets to Madison Square Garden where the Rangers played. So, while so many of my friends would go to Yankee Stadium or the Polo Grounds to watch the Yankees and Giants play (As I mentioned earlier, I did go to a few baseball games, and my idol was Mickey Mantle), my favorite sport was hockey because there was constant movement and, at any time, a fight would break out. Plus, seeing these players close-up with missing front teeth left me with many memories.

Flash forward to 1994 when the announcement is made in the local newspaper that a minor league hockey team was moving to Tallahassee for the 1994-95 season. On the day that ticket sales began, I bought season tickets for Harriet and me right above the penalty box. This gave us a completely unobstructed view of the ice and you get to hear conversation that you never hear on TV, or anyplace else in the arena for that matter. Before entering the penalty box, players would exchange observations and opinions. We learned new words, and foreign language words, if you know what I mean. We had these season tickets for the seven years of the team's stay in Tallahassee.

We met the players, had them to our home, attended their weddings and children's' births, and even went to Minneapolis for a player's wedding. We followed the team when it was on the road, and generally made friends with players, coaches and staff, a few of whom we remain in touch with to this day.

Over the seven-year history of the Tallahassee Tiger Sharks, Harriet and I collected pucks, sticks, pictures, team jersey logo patches, and other forms of collectibles and memorabilia. In total, we amassed quite a collection worth several thousands of dollars. Along with three other couples who also had season tickets, we formed an informal club we called the "Rink Rats." One of Rink Rats even created a pin in the shape of a rat that he had trademarked, and had T-shirts made that had the rat design and Rink Rat embroidered below it. Harriet and I wore the T-shirt and pin proudly for each home game. I was so influenced by having a local team to root for, I even created a piece of jewelry, a pin I called the "Puck O' Luck"--a four-leaf clover in the shape of a hockey stick with four pucks as leaves. I sold these in Tallahassee, and for one year after the Tiger Sharks left, in Pensacola since this city also had a team in this league; I still have several pins stashed away in a box. It was a wonderful and memorable seven-year run.

Although the team moved on after the 2001 season, we nevertheless kept our collection intact. But as time passed, we began to realize that someday we will have to move, and what would become of this collection began to prey more and more on my mind.

One day in November of 2014, I was checking the hockey websites (I still do this from force of habit--once hooked, always hooked) and noted with great surprise that the league, now simply labeled the ECHL (a double-AA hockey league) was to have its annual all-star game in Orlando, Florida. I went to the website directory and got the email address of the person who seemed to be the most logical in handling items of this type, and sent her an email noting what we had. Sure enough, a couple of days later, I received a response in which she said that we could meet at the host hotel and we could deliver the memorabilia to the front desk.

We bought two tickets to the game, and Harriet and I boxed up all of the items in our collection, except a few pieces that were of interest only to the National Hockey League. On the day of the game, we drove to Orlando, dropped off the 12 boxes of collectibles and then found this lady and told her what we had delivered to the hotel's front desk. We exchanged mobile phone numbers and she said she would get in touch with us during the game.

During intermission at the game, we met her again and she gave each of us a bag of all-star memorabilia. She said this was strange considering we were giving away so many items-- including over 200 hockey pucks--while the gift bag contained more memorabilia including a hockey puck, but it was her and the league's way of thanking us for our "generous donation."

Harriet and I felt good that our collection was now where we believed it belonged, but a few days later, after the league officials returned to headquarters and after looking at the hundreds of pucks, sticks, etc., she told us that the league didn't have the proper facility to house such a collection, but that she was sending the entire collection to the Hockey Hall of Fame in Toronto, Canada. Needless to say, we were ecstatic.

A few days later, we received an email from the HHOF advising that it now had our collection and that we would be receiving a full acknowledgement when the items were inventoried. Evidently, the HHOF receives donations from leagues, teams, players and occasionally fans, but ours was among the most elaborate from the fans category. I then told the representative that I had a few additional items from NHL teams, including three one-of-a-kind items. The HHOF was so thrilled that its archivist gave us its FedEx courier number so we could send these items at no cost to us.

About a month after the HHOF took delivery of our collection, we received a letter thanking us for our donation, noting that our "contribution helps (the HHOF) preserve and display a wonderful collection of hockey artifacts to over 300,000 guests annually." Our collection was assigned accession or inventory numbers (Nos. 316-122 to 316-130 and 316-149 to 316-152) similar to the way a library catalogs books. We also received multi-page inventories clearly identifying each of the 250 or so items we donated. These accession numbers are used to identify the item and source of donation, so, as famed baseball manager Casey Stengel used to say, "You could look it up."

Thus, our entire hockey collection amassed over the years now resides with and is the property of the HHOF. Harriet and I are more than thrilled that our efforts in building this collection have been rewarded by the knowing that it has a permanent home in the place most befitting of all, and is available for the visiting public to see. Harriet and I are in the Hockey Hall of Fame!!

Harriet got to be such a fan that, for one of our wedding anniversaries, she gave me a puck in an acrylic case. On that puck, she had printed on one side "Happy 29th Anniversary 7-18-00" and on the other side "My Love Always, Me" with a heart drawn around the Me. Now, I call this romantic commitment.

I have a few other hockey items that are not considered memorabilia. One is a replica Jerry Cheevers goalie mask. What makes this an interesting item is the story behind the original mask. It bears a stitch pattern, and came about after a puck hit Cheevers in the face during practice. He went to the dressing room, and was followed by the coach, who found Cheevers enjoying a beer and smoking a cigarette. The coach told Cheevers, who wasn't injured, to get back on the ice. In jest, the team trainer drew a stitch mark on his mask. After that, any time he was similarly struck, he would have a new stitch-mark drawn on. The mask became one of the most recognized of the era. The original now belongs to Cheevers' grandson. My replica makes for a great Halloween mask.

There's a large picture of the Stanley Cup-winning Tampa Bay Lightning for 2004; a large Lightning cup-winning banner; a large replica Stanley Cup; and a model of the Stanley Cup won by the Colorado Avalanche in 1996. This is what's left of my hockey stuff.

I have three major league baseballs, one each signed by Pete Rose, Brooks Robinson and Spec Richardson. You may have heard of Rose and Robinson; Spec Richardson was the general manager of the Houston Astros and San Francisco Giants. But the value of this ball is not in the signature; it's in the logo. He signed a ball bearing the logo for the 1994 World Series. What's so special about this? There was no world series in 1994; the players went on strike and the series was cancelled.

I have miniature football helmet signed by famed FSU head coach Bobby Bowden; a signed photo of the University of Florida's Heisman-winning quarterback Tim Tebow and head coach Urban Meyer; and a signed soccer ball from the Tallahassee Scorpions, a minor league indoor team that lasted two years. To give you an idea of how fast this fad faded, the attendance for the first game was over 6,000; by the time this Eastern Indoor Soccer League team folded at the end of its second year, attendance was less than 600.

Finally, I have a replica football Coaches Trophy of the national champion University of Florida in 2006. I think my youngest daughter and son-in-law, both UF graduates, want this. I'll keep that in mind.

15. What is really important in life

I think there are three distinct periods in our lives. Although there is some overlap, the three are: (1) the accumulatory, (2) the interactive, and (3) the reflective. In our youthful years, we accumulate--education, knowledge, etc. However, because we are accumulating at such a great speed, we are generally too wrapped up in this gathering process to truly appreciate what it is that we are accumulating.

After formal schooling and the accumulation of necessary skills and knowledge, we transition to the interactive period. We enter the work force and marry, interacting with family, friends, acquaintances, co-workers, peers, etc. With so many obligations inherent in this period, there's no time for taking stock--to stop and smell the roses, so to speak.

When our children move on with their lives and we leave the workforce, we move into the reflective period, looking back and taking stock on what we've accumulated and with whom we interacted in this great journey that is life. It is time to sum up the totality of the first two periods, instilling in us wisdom to advise others and bring contentment to ourselves. If we've been fortunate, we have passed "GO" and we did collect that $200.

At the beginning of this book, I said we are all collectors at heart. If we see something that catches our eyes, we want to have it. So, generally speaking, we proceed along the path of life gathering stuff. Perhaps some of this stuff will look good in our homes; perhaps looking at some of this stuff will bring back a memory or two; perhaps some of this stuff is a personal or precious keepsake that you inherited and has been in your family for generations; perhaps we want some of this stuff just to have it. Whatever the reason may be--assuming there is a reason--we continue to gather stuff. Why? Because whether we are aware of it or not, we are collecting memories; objects that remind us of other times and other places. Each one captures a meaningful event or a precious, private moment.

As we accumulate this stuff, we are usually too busy in our lives to take stock of what it is we really need or want. We spend precious little time choosing between needs and wants; yet we know there is a stark difference between the two. If we are fortunate to have the resources, this choice is given that much less consideration.

But as we get older and tend to take stock of our lives, we begin to focus on what we have and start to ask ourselves whether what we have is what we need or what we want. Have we spent a lifetime gathering stuff that meant something at one time, but is junk today? Can we separate the "what I need" from the "what I want?" There are those who suffer from separation anxiety whenever the thought crosses their mind that someday they will have to sell, give away or throw away objects they have long possessed. But taking stock of one's holdings and separating the needs from the wants is a decision that must eventually be made. As we get older, we must adjust to the current times; there's no alternative to doing this. There are things we did as young adults that we simply can't do in our senior years. Life is, after all, a series of continuing adjustments.

There is a wonderful quote, the author of which is unknown, that should remind us of what is truly important: "The happiest people don't have the best of everything; they just make the best of everything they have." In other words, it isn't about simply getting things you don't have, it's about giving thanks for the things you do have.

The quest for material objects doesn't necessarily bring happiness. Happiness is from within; love for and of family; good friends; a reputation for honesty and compassion; a sense of accomplishment; pride in a job well done; and on and on-- none of these requires the accumulation or possession of objects, or stuff. But objects do allow us to take a moment to kick back our heels and remember.

As you may recall, I started this narrative by discussing my pictures and ego room. The many pictures, objects--just things- -are important to me, not for their intrinsic value, but because of the memories they evoke. My family comes first. My wife, children and grandchildren give me all the reasons I need for a life of pure enrichment. My ego room contains items that remind me of my professional life, and the people whose lives touched me and, hopefully, whose lives I have touched along the way. And to have been recognized by my peers for a job well done is simply icing on the cake.

In our travels, my wife and I have accumulated some stuff. We collect magnets from every port and city we have visited, and we will continue to gather magnets in our future travels. Not because we need them; just because we want them as reminders. As I said earlier, we are all collectors.

I also collect books that I've read, but with the advent of handheld readers on which I can download books, this collection has just about reached its peak. Someday these books will be donated to the local library.

Now that I am in my 70s, I think about the day that will come when we must move, most likely to a smaller home closer to one of our children. Although this is several years down the road, when that day arrives, my wife and I will have to decide what to do with our personal property. As I said earlier, there are three choices for each item: keep it, give it away or throw it away. If an item remains valuable to us or our children, we'll keep it. If it is something that someone else can make better use of and my children don't want it, we'll give it away. And if it is in the pure junk category, we'll toss it.

We've already given away our valuable and voluminous collection of hockey memorabilia. It took over 20 years to amass this collection, and these items--once very precious to me--were becoming a burden, making me wonder what would happen to it when the time to relocate approached. Fortunately, we found an ultimate donor, and the donation to the Hockey Hall of Fame in Toronto was a logical and most appropriate place.

Assorted knick-knacks will be given to Goodwill, a senior citizens center, or other facility that takes such donations to make the lives of others a bit more pleasant and richer.

Items that my wife and I want to keep in the family will be given to our children. If they don't want them, they will be moved to the "give it away" category--and join all the other stuff that's not in the "keep it" category.

It's a trite but true statement that bears repeating; life is a collection of memories. But it isn't necessary for each memory to be represented by an object, or stuff. A picture is worth a thousand words of memories. So where a picture brings back a memory, we will keep the picture and probably ditch the object that was initially purchased to capture that same memory.

This will reduce the stress associated with object removal, and allow me to keep this type of memorabilia where it truly and lastingly belongs, in my mental memory bank.

Having too much of anything can be a burden. I am reminded of the adage keep it simple, stupid. Of course, this doesn't mean that complicating our lives with extraneous matter is a sign of stupidity; it does, however, mean that extraneous matters can complicate what is otherwise easy.

There is another quote that should be a rule and guide: "God grant me the serenity to accept the things I cannot change, the courage to change the things I can, and the wisdom to know the difference." If only we--I--took more time to reflect on Reinhold Niebuhr's words of wisdom!

In the last analysis, it's the simple things that enrich our lives; the "stop and smell the roses" things that are truly meaningful. Perhaps that, in order to fully understand that it's the simple things that are most valuable, it is necessary to gain experience that can only come through the passage of time.

Randy Pausch said it best: "Experience is what you get when you don't get what you want." If you go through life always getting what you want, how do you learn to deal with failure? We learn, not from our successes, but from our failures. Success means little or nothing if there is no failure to compare it with; put another way, only through failure can you appreciate the value of success. That which doesn't kill you, makes you stronger. Or it certainly should. The reality is that failure either makes you weaker or stronger; ultimately, it's your choice, and yours alone, to make. I know that failure has made me stronger; it's really not a choice if you want to survive and prosper.

Wisdom is gained through experience; everything we experience helps mold character. It is our experiences that make us who we are, and make life the rich and glorious journey that it can be if there is a willingness to take charge and accept the responsibilities and effort that must be put forth.

When I was younger, I noticed that older people tended to complain more and become grouchy. I vowed never to be like that, so I try to catch myself when I complain and whine about something I see or hear. Harriet is also helpful in pointing out my whine-and-grouch moments. But I think I know why this happens to older people. As we age, we see the young making similar mistakes to those we made when we were young and, by internalization, I think we want them to learn early on from us older folks so that they won't repeat the mistakes we made back then. Although well-intended, I think that ultimately, this is a futile effort; they will simply have to learn the way we did--through trial and error, and by making mistakes. This is what experience is all about, and instills wisdom.

So, what keeps me busy now? With the addition of OLLI, I keep up with my two families via Facebook and email, in addition to our visits; I play word games on Facebook to keep my mind sharp and maintain a competitive edge; there's our travel schedule; visiting with friends; writing; going to the gym; neighborhood walks; and just taking time to stop and smell the roses and relishing the joys of a less hectic, less stressful life. Nothing wrong with that, eh? In other words, I'm trying to make my life just as it was when I was working, only without the work. This certainly makes sense to me.

Finally, I think we all contemplate at one time or another--especially as we get older--what kind of legacy we want to leave behind. For me, this is easy. I keep a quote on my desk; it's a quote I came across many years ago. It says: "A hundred years from now, it will not matter what my bank account was, the sort of house I lived in, or the kind of car I drove...but the world may be different because I was important in the life of a child." This is a great quote; it makes me realize that what's truly important is not material possessions, but how important someone is in the life of others.

This is a most valuable lesson, and is a good a place as any to end this brief book; hopefully, more will follow.

IV. Endnote

The growing emphasis on ancestry tells me that people are becoming more and more interested in, and fascinated with, our past. We want to know about our lineage; who our great-grandparents were; who their parents were; as far back as we can go and records can take us.

What better way to leave a legacy for your children, their children--generation after generation--than writing your life story. The only way they will really know who you are is if you tell them in your own words. No filter, no interpretive gloss. All of your strengths and weaknesses. All of your trials and tribulations. Warts and all.

As I said in my 2012 memoir, no one knows your life story better than you. So, why not write it? You might think you have nothing to say; you've led an uneventful life. I used to think that way, until I actually sat down, wrote an outline, and started typing on my computer. Once I started putting words on paper, the words flowed, as if guided by an unexplainable force. It seemed I couldn't type fast enough. That force is the strength of your memory bank.

After more than 175,000 words covering almost 500 pages in two books, I have now told my life story up to this point. I hope that I have convinced you to write yours. Each of us lives a unique life; no two people have identical experiences. I found the hardest part of this effort was actually sitting down and beginning the journey of writing my life experiences.

Here's your assignment: make it a point to set aside some time (you can do it; if I can, you can) and sit down and write an outline. Start with your early childhood, and proceed chronologically. I have no doubt the memories will flow faster and faster; you will find yourself writing faster and faster. When you start typing, your fingers will glide across the keyboard, and you'll be on your way. And when you're done, you'll feel a sense of great pride and accomplishment. Deservingly so.

So, what are you waiting for? Go get a pen, some paper, and begin what will be a great experience for you and a treasure for your family. Write your life story...up to now.

Printed in the United States
By Bookmasters